# Hermit Crabs

## CAROL FRISCHMANN

*Hermit Crab*
Project Team
Editor: Thomas Mazorlig
Copy Editor: Ellen Bingham
Indexer: Elizabeth Walker
Design Concept: Leah Lococo Ltd.,
Stephanie Krautheim
Design Layout: Patricia Escabi

TFH Publications
President/CEO: Glen S. Axelrod
Executive Vice President: Mark E. Johnson
Publisher: Christopher T. Reggio
Production Manager: Kathy Bontz

TFH Publications, Inc.
One TFH Plaza
Third and Union Avenues
Neptune City, NJ 07753

Discovery Communications, LLC. Book Development Team: Marjorie
Kaplan, President and General Manager, Animal Planet Media/ Kelly
Day, Executive Vice President and General Manager, Discovery
Commerce/ Elizabeth Bakacs, Vice President, Licensing and Creative/
JP Stoops, Director, Licensing/ Betsy Ferg, Design Director, Licensing/
Bridget Stoyko, Associate Art Director, Licensing

Printed and bound in China.
12 13 14 15   3 5 7 9 8 6 4 2

Library of Congress Cataloging-in-Publication Data
Frischmann, Carol.
   Hermit crabs / Carol Frischmann.
      p. cm. – (Animal planet pet care library)
   Includes bibliographical references and index.
   ISBN 978-0-7938-3708-3 (alk. paper)
   1. Hermit crabs as pets. I. Title.
   SF459.H47F75 2011
   639'.67–dc22
                          2010048737

*The Leader in Responsible Animal Care for Over 50 Years!*®
www.tfh.com

# Table of Contents

# Chapter 1

## Why I Adore My

# Hermit Crab

The unusual habits of hermit crabs fascinate aspiring naturalists and outdoors enthusiasts because of the adaptations they have made to their environment. Artists appreciate the beauty of the seashells this creature chooses as his mobile home. Practical people who work long hours love that the hermit crab does not require hours of attention and three walks each day. What starts as curiosity about hermit crabs usually develops into admiration for their habits, habitation, and wholly interesting bodies. Let's look more closely at the characteristics of the animal that inspires "crabby people" to say "I adore my hermit crabs."

*The pet hermit crabs covered in this book live on land, but they return to the sea to lay their eggs.*

### The Allure of Hermit Crabs

Not only do hermit crabs have an ancient heritage, even older than the dinosaurs, but they also have some advantages over traditional pets. However, their needs are specific, because of their ties to both land and water. No matter how you look at hermit crabs, they are unusual, fascinating, and definitely nothing like dogs or cats. Let's look further at what makes some people go crab crazy.

### Ties to the Past

Hermit crabs are part of a group of animals that evolved before the dinosaurs. The name of this group, *arthropod*, comes from the Greek words for joint and foot. The parts of a hermit crab that can extend beyond his shell have a tough, jointed covering that looks and works like a knight's suit of armor.

### Ties to Water and Land

The clan called crabs, including the hermit crabs, varies in color and size and occupies many different environments. Some crabs never leave the water. Some crabs never leave the land. The common pet hermit crab lives his adult life on land but starts life as an egg in the ocean.

### Unusual

Almost nothing about hermit crabs is ordinary—to us humans, anyway. They carry their homes wherever they go. When hermit crabs grow, they hunt for new shell homes. A lack of fur is another characteristic that distinguishes hermit crabs from traditional pets. Parents might consider crabs as pets for children who are allergic to dogs and cats.

## Beautiful

Small and unusual animals are often overlooked by potential pet owners. Hermit crabs are different from a Persian cat or a Great Dane, but they are beautiful animals nevertheless.

## Suitable for Small Spaces and Busy Lifestyles

Although hermit crabs require specific conditions to remain healthy and active, they can suit people who have small spaces and busy lives. Unlike dogs and cats, hermit crabs are not dependent on a person for companionship. Although they can be solitary creatures, you also can keep several hermit crabs together.

Hermit crabs don't mind if your daily schedule is irregular—they don't require a strict schedule. So long as you offer food and water daily, the precise schedule is not important. Neither do they require walks or daily play. Given space and opportunities for climbing and digging, hermit crabs exercise themselves.

If you live in a small space, hermit crabs offer a unique advantage. You can structure your hermit crab habitat (or

"crabitat") and the number of crabs you keep to fit your available space. Another excellent characteristic of pet hermit crabs is that nearby neighbors are unlikely to complain about noise, because hermit crabs make only a few quiet sounds.

Perhaps the best attribute, described by hobbyists who call themselves "crabbers," is that individual hermit crabs have definite "personalities."

No matter what first attracted you to these fascinating creatures, there's much to know before you can take care of your hermit crab with confidence and efficiency. Reading this book is an excellent beginning.

This slim volume explains what hermit crabs are, how their bodies work, what their habits and requirements are, and where you can go for more information. At the end,

*Hermit crabs are crustaceans, a group of animals that also includes other crabs, lobsters, shrimps, barnacles, and pill bugs.*

# The Hermit Crab's Classification

This book is about the *Coenobita*, or land hermit crab.

**Invertebrates**

**Phylum:  Arthropoda (insects, crabs, spiders)**

**Class: Crustacea (crabs, shrimp, barnacles)**

**Infraorder:  Anomura (crab-like animals)**

**Superfamily: Paguroidea (hermit crabs, stone crabs, king crabs)**

**Family: Coenobitidae (land hermit crabs)**

**Family: Paguridae (right-handed marine hermit crabs)**

**Family: Diogenidae (left-handed marine hermit crabs)**

**Family: Paraguridae (deepwater hermit crabs)**

you'll find a list of resources, websites, blogs, online groups, and videos that will give you even more information about hermit crabs and connect you to other crab-loving people.

## What Is a Hermit Crab?

Hermit crabs are relatives of the crabs you eat. Instead of growing its own shell, though, the hermit crab borrows one. A hermit crab's soft abdomen and tail remain anchored inside his borrowed shell. The head, legs, and pincers can move out of the shell when it is safe and withdraw into the shell when the crabs sense danger. Over time, hermit crabs outgrow their borrowed shell and have to change shells. Sometimes the crabs change shells for other reasons. This behavior fascinates almost everyone who discovers it. To learn more about the hermit crab, we need to look at its place in the animal kingdom.

## Hermit Crab's Scientific Classification

The hermit crab's place in a "scientific classification" is like a family genealogy or family tree. This classification tells us about the characteristics of the hermit crab—including body arrangement and functions, which define the hermit crab's needs. If we understand the crab's needs, we can do a better job of meeting them.

In addition to the land hermit crabs, there exists three families of marine hermit crabs. Some marine crabs live in shallow water, some live in tide pools, and some you would have to snorkel or dive to see. Those marine hermit crabs are sometimes included in saltwater aquaria, requiring a very different environment from that of the land hermit crabs that are our focus.

Now that we know the hermit crab's position in the scientific family tree, let's start at the top of the "The Hermit Crab's Classification." As we move from top to bottom, you will learn increasingly specific details of the hermit crab's body plan and internal systems. We'll focus on the things you need to know to take good care of your pet, rather than the details of each group.

### Separating Male Crabs from Female Crabs

Male and female crabs usually can be distinguished by the larger male claw size. This difference can be explained by the use of this claw for defending territory and fighting as well as in courtship displays. However, even for mature crabs, differentiating male from female can be difficult, especially when they are in their borrowed shells.

## What a Crab Does With Five Pairs of Legs

| Leg pair | Common name | Scientific term | Use |
|---|---|---|---|
| 1 | claws or pincers | chelipeds | defense, balance, feeding, scooping water, shell selection |
| 2, 3 | walking legs | pereiopods | walking |
| 4, 5 | reduced walking legs | pleopods | fastening to the shell, grooming gills, removing waste from the shell |

### Invertebrates

When we stroke a dog or cat from head to tail, we can feel a backbone. Backbones are a main structure of their bodies as well as ours. Hermit crabs are members of a group called invertebrates, or animals without backbones. They support their bodies from the outside using an exoskeleton. One excellent aspect of hermit crab keeping is that "crabbers" have a chance to live with a creature whose body type is very different from our own.

### Arthropods

Invertebrates are divided into several groups, including arthropods, which contain most species on the planet. As arthropods, hermit crabs are related to nearly nine-tenths of all known animal species.

Hermit crabs share the arthropod body plan, which features a hard exoskeleton and jointed appendages. The hermit crab body is mostly abdomen. Hermit crabs have small heads, with their eyes attached by eyestalks instead of being protected by surrounding structures. They have paired antennae and special mouthparts that scientists call maxillipeds.

### Close Relatives of the Hermit Crab

Within the arthropods, hermit crabs belong to a group called crustaceans. The crustaceans also include "true" crabs (not hermit crabs), lobsters, and crayfish—creatures that are important sources of food. Describing what distinguishes the hermit crab from these cousins doesn't help us with this short book's purpose: to provide information for understanding and caring for your hermit crab. However, much of the research that applies to hermit crabs comes from the study of their cousins who are important to the seafood industry.

Anomura is a subgroup of crustaceans. Some of the 1,500 to 2,000 species of Anomura are hermit crabs. Anomura have two or three pairs of visible walking legs. The fourth or fifth pair of legs is smaller, less developed, and hidden under the body. Within Anomura is the "superfamily" Pagurioidea, which includes all hermit crabs, marine and land. All hermit crabs have one thing in common: They use empty snail shells as their "mobile homes."

The superfamily includes marine hermit crabs that require a saltwater environment, including the Paguridae, the Diogenidae, and the deepwater hermit crabs, the Paraguridae. This book does not focus on these groups.

The land hermit crabs, the *Coenobita*, part of superfamily Pagurioidea, are the animals we'll be discussing from this point forward. The *Coenobita* live near water, rather than in it. Scientists, hermit crab suppliers, zoo and aquarium keepers, and "serious crabbers" use these Latin scientific names to be clear about which group or species of animals is being discussed.

## *Coenobita:* A Quick Overview

The *Coenobita*, or land hermit crabs, have five pairs of legs, each pair adapted for a special job. One pair is a set of claws (or pincers), with one pincer much larger than the other. Hermit crabs can withdraw entirely inside their shell, blocking the opening with these claws, the first leg pair. Leg pairs two and three are walking legs. Pairs four and five grip the rings inside the borrowed shell that protects the soft abdomen.

Hermits' organs perform essential body functions. Most organs lay inside the long abdomen, which is twisted into the protective shell's spiral. The brain, located in the head, directs all crab activities using a controlling network that extends throughout the crab's body. Oxygen enters and carbon dioxide leaves the body through a system of modified gills and gaps in the hard body covering.

Hermits can be male or female, and they reproduce at the water's edge. Young crabs hatch in the water, looking nothing like their parents, and undergo a series of complete body shape changes before they assume their adult form.

Hermit crabs range throughout the world, but most come from tropical climates. Within the range, they live

## Regenerating Legs

When a crab's leg breaks—say because a predator grabs one—the hermit crab is capable of regrowing the leg. The lost limb regenerates partially before the molt—called a limb bud—but usually does not complete formation until after the crab's next molt.

Sometimes, limb loss speeds up the molt. Of the hermit crabs that *autotomize* (cast off) a limb, 25 percent molt within 21 days. Reallocation of food and energy to the regrowth of a limb, though, negatively affects the crab's overall health.

*Hermit crabs live in the abandoned shells of other animals and need to move to larger shells as they grow larger themselves.*

in different habitats, each species of *Coenobita* having evolved to survive in one specific habitat.

Crabs scavenge dead plants and animals, feeding and going about activities mainly at night. Although crabs recognize each other, they don't seek social interaction. They can be aggressive when frightened or challenged, but they rarely vocalize. When they do, their chirps are relatively quiet.

### Looking at the Hermit Crab's Exterior

Now that we have some general ideas about the hermit crab, let's look more closely.

### The Shell

Much about the hermit crab's behavior and body type comes from its use of another animal's shell as its home.

Starting with the outside, if we can look away from the shell for a moment, notice that the hermit crab's body has a left and a right side, each a mirror image of the other. Each side has five legs, two antennae, and one eye. Not all animals are this way. Think starfish, for example.

### The Outer Covering

The hermit crab bodys' tough outer covering, the exoskeleton (*exo* is Greek meaning "outside"), protects everything except the abdomen and tail, which coil inside the borrowed shell. The exoskeleton supports the crab and provides a place to attach muscles.

The exoskeleton is made of protein and a material called chitin, and this forms a strong, rigid, lightweight, and waterproof covering. Yet the skeleton remains flexible at the joints. If you have eaten whole crab, lobster, or crayfish, then you've cracked the chitinous exoskeleton to get to the part that you eat, the muscle.

Chitin is a long strand of sugar, reinforced with lengths of protein. The microscopic lengths of protein are oriented to provide strength where the skeleton is most stressed. These strands of protein do what the double stitching and pockets do on your jeans. If you look at your jeans, you'll see that many seams are double stitched to make the jeans stronger. Pockets reinforce the jeans seat. The linked proteins reinforce the crab's outer skeleton in that same way.

### The Head
A single piece of tough chitin covers the hermit crab's head and part of the chest, or thorax. This piece of the exoskeleton, sometimes called a carapace, protects the head and breathing organs.

### The Appendages: Feelers, Legs, and Mouthparts
Your hermit crabs' appendages—working parts that extend from the main part of their bodies—are very special. These body parts are used in signaling, fighting, feeding, defense, and mating. Because these parts are jointed and strong, they can be precisely controlled by the hermit crab.

Two pairs of feelers, or antennae, are on the crab's head. The longer pair gathers information to supplement the

eyes, helping the hermit crab orient by feeling what is ahead. The shorter antennae provide the senses of smell and taste—the same information you get from your nose and tongue. The head of the crab also contains jaws (sometimes called mandibles) and small movable mouthparts specialized for gathering and handling food.

### The Legs
Hermit crabs are decapods (*deca* means "ten" and *pod* means "foot"), which means that they have five pair of legs. Let's consider more about each pair of legs.

The first legs, or claws, are large and important. The larger left claw

## Making Crabs Crabby
Each appendage collects information about the crab's environment at all times. Be careful not to restrict the motion of its appendages. This frightens the crab. When frightened, crabs will pinch with their claws. This is their way of saying, "Hey, let go of me! I can't see, smell, or understand what's happening when you keep my exploring parts from moving."

The enlarged left claw helps a hermit crab defend himself. It can both pinch an attacker and block the opening of the shell.

is for defense. Not only can the crab wave the claw at predators, but when withdrawing entirely into his shell, he can also use this claw to block the opening, closing out the invader. Crabs also grip tree limbs with their left claw. Finally, the left claw helps the crab keep his balance. Crabs move their left claw much as kids would use their arms to balance while walking on narrow ledges.

Crabs use the much smaller right claw to collect and pass food to the mouth, as well as scoop water for drinking and cleaning the shell.

Crabs also use their claws to find appropriate shells. They estimate shell size measuring against their claws, and inspect the shell's condition by turning it over and passing their claws over the surface, ensuring that it has no holes or cracks.

## Looking Inside the Crab

To understand what our hermit crab needs, we must peek inside, at how the interior parts of the crab's body are organized (the anatomy) and how those parts work together (the physiology). Together, anatomy and physiology describe the crab's systems for gathering and using food to support his growth, movement, and reproduction.

### Sensory Organs and Nerves

The hermit crab's brain is located at the front and at the top of the head. The three parts of the brain act as a unit to start and control behavior.

A nerve cord runs from the brain along the length of the hermit

# Crabby People: The Junkins Family

There are five Junkins humans, three cats, a dog, two hamsters, and four hermit crabs. They met their first hermit crab on a beach vacation: Someone left it on their porch. When they visited a pet store to learn how to care for the dying crab, the Junkins family took four new crabs home with them. Here is what they have to say about crabs as pets:

Claire, 7 years old, loves the family pets. "The best thing about crabs is that they tickle," she says. What surprised Claire most is that crabs can feel vibrations made by fingers tapping on a tabletop.

"Pick them up gently, so they don't pinch with their claws," Claire says. "The worst thing about crabs is that they can pinch." She advises getting a large habitat for your crabs.

Crosby, 15, likes crabs' liveliness. He worries when the crabs are not active. "I don't know what's going on with them," he says.

Derek, 17, likes that hermit crabs are quiet. "What surprised me," he said, "is that they eat almost anything—including a cage mate if the crabitat is too crowded."

Doug, the Junkins dad, likes to feel the hermit crabs walk up his arm. He thinks of crabs as perky pets. He hates cleaning the crabitat but loves to watch the crabs change their shells.

Mom, Laurie, likes hermit crabs because they are low-maintenance but have so much personality. Like Crosby, Mom worries, when the crabs are molting, whether they are warm enough and whether the crabitat has enough humidity to make them comfortable.

"Be careful what you name your crabs," the Junkinses advise. They named one of the crabs "Jenny" after a personal-trainer friend. Turns out, Jenny the crab pushes the other three crabs around the same way Jenny the trainer pushes her trainees. Go figure.

crab's body through each of the approximately 19 segments in the body. Each segment has a small bundle of nerve tissue, called a ganglion, that controls the activities in that segment and any appendage, such as antennae or legs. That ganglion also collects information sensed by the segment and sends that information to the brain through the nerve cord.

Hermit crabs have compound eyes, consisting of many light-sensitive units, on mobile eye stalks. Some species of crabs see in color and have binocular vision from the overlapping visual fields of the two eyes. But this isn't the total story about crab vision.

Crab's eyes are different from ours. Each compound eye is made up of many light-receiving units, or ommatidia. Each ommatidium receives light from one spot on the visual field, some of the light falling on its neighbors. Because of this overlap, the hermit crab's compound eyes detect movement across a large field of vision. Because sensory organs can't be good at everything, the cost of this movement-sensitive vision is a hazier image vision than humans have.

This vision works well for crabs, though. The most important function for their vision is to alert them to predators' approach so that they can withdraw into their shells for protection. (Tip: This ultra-sensitivity to movement is why you should approach your crab slowly.)

If you think about the position of the crab's eyes (above the body), it makes sense that they have bristles on the antennae and walking legs.

Just as dogs and cats have whiskers, and blind people use canes, to collect information about their environment, crabs' bristles and hairs help these animals locate food, mates, and predators.

These hairs do much more than whiskers or canes, though. Crabs' hairs are sensitive to air- and water-borne chemicals that humans might detect as odors. Other types of hermit crab hair receptors sense touch, sound, and vibration. Scientists believe that crabs that migrate have receptors to detect Earth's magnetic fields, as insects and birds do. As you can see, "invisible" receptors on the bristles help the crab learn much about his environment.

## Muscles and Movement

Body movement is a segment-by-segment event. Each of a hermit crab's muscles is attached to a specific segment of a limb. As we already know, each segment's limb is controlled by the ganglion in that segment. This means that nerve impulses travel a short distance. Crabs move their paired limbs in sequence by segment. This segmented body plan allows efficient, quick, and precise motion that we sometimes see as a rapid skittering.

The hermit crab can also make complicated combinations of movements requiring coordination across segments. Examples include internal organ contractions, such as those of the gut, and motions we can see, such as the crab waving a claw while retreating from a predator,

and moving his antennae to examine what's behind him.

## Feeding, Digestion, and Excretion

One scientist describes hermit crabs as "omnivorous detritivores"— meaning they eat animal and plant leftovers found most anywhere. Although hermit crabs eat many things, they can digest only small food particles. They use specially adapted feeding limbs to help them reduce the size of foods. These maxillipeds (from the Greek words for jaw and foot) hold the food while the jaws or mandibles cut and crush it.

Food enters through the mouth and moves into the gut, which extends from one end of the crab to the other. The first part of the gut grinds the food into smaller pieces. These tiny pieces pass into the center of the gut, which makes a digestive juice that breaks the food into the molecules the crab's body can use—proteins, carbohydrates, and fats.

## Blue-Green Blood?

Special proteins in the blood increase the ability of the blood to absorb oxygen. In cats and dogs, the protein is hemoglobin, which is red, and their blood is red in color. In crabs, the pigment is hemocyanin. Hemocyanin is the reason that crab *blood* (more correctly called hemolymph) is blue-green in color.

17

Why I Adore my Hermit Crab

Food that can't be digested moves to the end of the gut. The gut creates a membrane around the waste. Hermit crabs eliminate these feces through an anus located at the end of the tail.

Excretory organs for crabs' liquid waste sit at the base of the antennae. These glands open with a flap of cuticle. The fluid contains liquid organic waste, mostly ammonia, and excess water.

### Respiration

Respiration is a process that delivers oxygen to an animal's tissues and removes the carbon dioxide produced by the tissues' activities. Hermit crabs have a variety of structures that help them accomplish this vital function.

In hermit crabs, the gills are the major site of oxygen and carbon dioxide (or gas) exchange. The gills allow oxygen into the crab's body only when they are moist. Crabs store water in their borrowed seashell and use the water to bathe their gills to keep them moist enough for gas exchange.

In addition to the gills, hermit crabs have structures that are called lungs but that are not much like human lungs in their shape and that do not accomplish breathing as we think of it. Nevertheless, these structures contain thin, folded membranes through which the crab can absorb oxygen and give carbon dioxide back to the environment. These thin membranes lie under portions of the outer skeleton. The circulatory system moves the gases between the crab's gills, lungs, and other tissues.

### Circulation

The job of the heart and circulatory system is to deliver oxygen, nutrients, and hormones through the body of the crab and to collect the carbon dioxide and wastes from the other systems and dispose of them. Maintaining the correct amount of water and other body liquid chemistries is a part of this system.

A hermit crab's heart lies under the carapace. The heart contracts, pumping blood out into one of the

## Breathe Easy

As a keeper of hermit crabs, there is an important reason for maintaining a humid environment and access to water at all times for your crab. When your crab has a dry environment and not enough water, the crab reacts as you do when your lungs are congested. You feel you cannot get enough air. Your activities are restricted. You feel sick. Your focus is on restoring your ease of breathing. This is how a crab feels in an environment that is too dry.

providing adequate warmth for your crab. How to do this is discussed in Chapter 2.

## Hormones, Growth, and Reproduction

Crabs have hormones, just as dogs, cats, and humans do. Hormones control several functions in your crab's body, including reproduction and molting, the process that allows for your pet's growth. Although as a crab hobbyist, you will not encounter reproduction, you will need to provide the resources for molts many times during his long life.

### Hormones

The endocrine system produces and regulates hormones. Cells belonging to this system abide in the brain and ganglia, near the heart, in a special organ called the "Y" organ, and in the reproductive organs. The reproductive organs, ovaries, and testes are located inside the crab's body near the top. You can't point to one spot and say, "Here's where the hormones originate."

### Reproduction

Reproductive hormones cause reproduction. In young crabs, these hormones cause the development of the reproductive system. In adult crabs, reproductive hormones act on

five to seven arteries. The blood flows past the oxygen-collection organs, picks up the fresh oxygen, and moves through the tissues, dropping off the nutrition and oxygen needed and collecting the gas and other wastes. The hemolymph (crab blood) collects in a series of vessels. Veins return it to the area near the gills to drop off carbon dioxide and pick up more oxygen.

Nerves control the crab's heart, which beats about 120 times per minute in a resting hermit crab. In addition to the heartbeat, normal body muscular contraction assists the flow of blood through the crab's body. These processes help maintain the crab's normal body temperature at about 73°F (23°C), much lower than a dog's 100.5°–102.5°F (38°–39.2°C). This lower body temperature underscores the importance of

19

Hermit crabs will feed on coconuts, but they cannot break open the shells themselves.

the organs in females and glands in males to make the sperm and eggs required to create new crabs.

## Molting

Crabs molt in order to grow. Because their exoskeletons are not expandable, the crab must split the old one, crawl out, and grow a new one. While the new exoskeleton grows, the crab must find a place to protect itself. Once hunkered down in a safe place, the crab preserves energy to do the hard biological work of developing an entirely new cuticle. The cuticle is a hard but lightweight exterior, similar to an insect's hard outer coating, made of protein and chitin.

During this time, the crab may remain buried in the deep section of the crabitat you've provided. Some crabbers move their molting crabs to a separate enclosure to ensure their safety and quiet.

Scientists call molting ecydysis. Controlled by hormones, molting begins when the crab swallows air or water, creating internal pressure against the exoskeleton, which splits. The crab crawls out.

At that time, the crab requires enough water to support its size increase. The growth must happen quickly, before a new cuticle develops and hardens. Although molting might seem to be a short process that takes place every once in awhile, molting defines the crab's entire life. Like most animals, crabs grow more in the early part of their lives. This results in more frequent molts at a younger age. As crabs age, they grow less and molt less frequently. The growth during each molt tends to decrease over time. The period between molts tends to increase each time. Understanding the molting process puts into perspective the importance of providing the right diet and moisture at all times.

Molting takes place in four stages:
- The crab's body prepares for molting.
- The naked crab hides and grows.
- The new skeleton completes formation.
- The crab rests and recharges.

## Looking at Crab Behavior

Although wild hermit crabs do not naturally "socialize" outside of mating, they do exhibit a wide variety of interesting behaviors. To access the experience of pet crab hobbyists, please refer to the websites and blogs listed in Resources at the end of this book.

From the science that has been done, we know that hermit crab behavior is a response to factors such as daylight, daily tides, the lunar cycle, and seasons. Research continues into the mysterious ways in which hermit crabs decide to migrate, select mates, and choose the direction to find what they're seeking.

## Eating and Drinking

Land crabs eat widely from the animals and plants in their natural habitats. Scientists have found that food odor is not the way crabs discover food more distant than a few yards (meters) away. Instead, based on their sight, crabs gather around other feeding crabs. Another study focused on food located within 6.6 feet (2 m) of crabs—more like the pet crab situation. Within that radius, odors guided hermit crabs through horizontal and vertical mazes.

However, within those same distances, the combination of sight and odor dramatically increased crabs' excitement over the food source. Scientists measured crab excitement by the rate at which crabs flick their antennae. The foods tested in the study included fruit, fish, and animal feces. (See the studies by Burggren in the References section for more detail).

If you consider the hermit crab's native environment, this makes sense. The zone between the water and the

21

## How Do Crabs Poop?

Crabs digest food and have waste left over. This waste is surrounded by a membrane before crabs push the feces through their anus. The problem is, the feces are outside the body but inside the protective spiral of the borrowed shell. Crabs remove the feces from the shell during the bathing and grooming processes. Although water must be available for many reasons for your crab, this is one of them.

A giant relative of the hermit crab, the coconut crab feeds on coconuts by breaking open the shell with his claws. This crab is only rarely available as a pet.

trees is the principal food-finding zone for the crabs. Not only is the area limited, but the changing tide means that food locations and time available are unpredictable. Relying on one crab's senses to find food is not efficient when compared with relying on all the other crabs to help find food. Scientists say the crabs are using social cues.

## Methods of Eating and Drinking

How individual crabs approach vegetation, fruits, insects, and carrion depends on the crab's body size and the liquid or solid state of the food. Large crabs hold fruits with the claws and pinch the flesh, and the shape of the closed claws forms a "cup" that receives the fluid squeezed from the fruit. The smaller legs and mouthparts take the small pieces of food or the juice to the mouth. Hermit crabs drink water in the same way they collect fruit juice.

When eating carrion or insects, the claw holds the food while the walking legs peel away small pieces. The largest land crab, *Birgus latro*, the coconut crab, crushes food with his claws. On some islands, this crab has been observed foraging in farmers' fields and attacking small domestic fowl. Scientists watching crabs in their native environments observe that similar-sized crabs eat faster when others are present. Individuals rarely interfere with similar-sized crabs. Large crabs have been observed using their walking legs to "flick" much smaller crabs away from a fruit.

## Recognizing Other Crabs

Social hierarchies that captive hermit crabs form do not occur in the wild. Field observations suggest that only few weak interactions occur among nonbreeding hermit crabs, with nonbreeding crabs coming together only around food sources.

Hermit crabs do recognize each other after exposure to each other for as little as 30 minutes. This capability allows captive crabs to have a "social life," informed by previous meetings. In the wild, this recognition plays a role in mate selection, defense of territory, and domination in the habitat. Experiments have shown that crabs can discriminate between at least two familiar individuals, including having knowledge of which was the winner and which the loser in a fight. For example, odor causes a fight-losing crab to hesitate before entering the burrow of a fight-winning crab.

## Molting Stages

| Stage | What Happens | What You Need to Know |
|-------|-------------|----------------------|
| Premolt (before the molt) | Calcium is reabsorbed and stored from the old cuticle. A new cuticle begins to form. | You won't see this happen. |
| Molt | The old skeleton is shed. The crab rapidly increases in size by soaking in freshwater. Sometimes crabs eat their old exoskeleton. | This process takes a matter of hours and is extremely stressful for your crab. Proper temperature, a supply of freshwater, and nutrients are critical. |
| Postmolt (after the molt) | The new skeleton hardens using the stored calcium, plus other nutrients from water and food. Muscles build more tissue. | The crab's stress continues. Quiet, plenty of food, and water are required. |
| Intermolt (between molts) | New tissues are completed and energy is rebuilt. The skeleton finishes hardening. The crab enters a period of slow growth, the *normal* period. | The interval between molts increases as your crab ages. |

FAMILY-FRIENDLY TIP

# Are Hermit Crabs Good Pets for a Child?

Frederic Frye thinks so. Dr. Frye wrote the book that has become the standard for keepers of invertebrates. When Frye was a small boy, he was obsessed with invertebrate such as spiders, scorpions, and crabs. Frye's mother never liked his pets but "accepted them so long as they were housed in escape-proof quarters." In addition, his mother insisted, "[my pets] were fed and cared for before I could expect to receive the same consideration from her. It was a remarkably wise and prescient policy that I have followed as a parent."

Frye grew up and earned advanced degrees in biological sciences and veterinary medicine, and was elected a Fellow in the Royal Society of Medicine. This well-respected scientist, veterinarian, and parent started by keeping crabs and their relatives as pets, which he continues to do to this day.

As you can conclude from Mother Frye's strict supervision of her obsessed small child, parents do need to check the crabs daily, not just rely on a child's assessment of the crabs' condition. What seems normal to a child might seem abnormal to an adult. What seems like a sufficient job of cleaning and tidying the crab enclosure to your child may not pass your sniff test. Checking your child's work may lead to some teachable moments and will ensure that the crabs are well cared for.

## Mating

As with most decapods, hermit crab sexes live separately and pair only briefly as adults. Because they are nocturnal, solitary, and spread throughout the habitat, the male and female must travel some distance to find one another. The travel direction and timing may be assisted by pheromones, attraction to intertidal zones or food sources, or lunar or tidal rhythms.

*Birgus latro* has been observed mating in the wild. Migration and reproductive behaviors of *Coenobita clypeatus* have been observed, but no actual mating. In both cases, the crabs were between molts, and abdomens extended partway from their shells to allow for the male to deposit the packet of sperm.

Male *Coenobita perlatus*, in courtship, uses his chelipeds (claws) to hold, tap, and stroke the appendages of the female. If mating occurs, the male uses his fifth pereiopods to transfer sperm packets. When the *Coenobita* female's eggs are ready to hatch, she moves to the water's edge and drops her eggs into the surf. Some species live miles from the sea. Scientists are still trying to answer how females know in which direction to walk.

## Grooming

Wild hermit crabs experience flies and mites as parasites, just as dogs and cats suffer from fleas and ticks. Grooming is an important way to remove parasites, food, dirt, and salt.

Grooming activity typically follows a sequence. The crab grooms his front more than his rear portions. As in feeding, the third maxillipeds have major grooming roles.

Hermit crabs are known to fight over desired shells. Usually, the smaller crab will vacate his shell and start hunting for another.

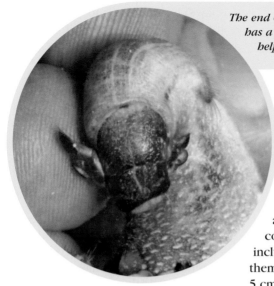

*The end of a hermit crab's abdomen has a structure called the telson that helps anchor the crab into his shell.*

predators and dryness, but it also serves as a place to nurture developing eggs.

In addition, some hermit crabs burrow while in their shells under leaf litter or cage substrate. Wild *Coenobita sinosa* burrow under dead vegetation and appear to hibernate during cold weather. Most hermit crabs, including *C. compressus*, bury themselves a half-inch to 2 inches (2 to 5 cm) deep prior to molting.

Eyestalks are a particular focus of grooming. The crabs move the eyestalk downward, hooking one or both of the third maxillipeds over it. The crab rubs the mouthpart "combs" over the eyestalk. Similarly, the crab grooms his antennules. Crabs groom their claws and legs by moving them over one another.

Field observations emphasize the value of water as a cleaning agent for hermit crabs. Following rains (or when captive crabs enter their water bowls), grooming activities are much more vigorous. Ensure that your crab has access to salt and freshwater at all times for grooming.

## Burrowing

Hermit crabs use their adopted shell as a mobile burrow. Not only does the shell provide protection from

## Aggression

Crabs signal aggression through body posture—chelipeds raised, held widely apart, and open.

Occasionally, during fights, a defender may leave his shell if it is being turned by an opponent. In fact, sometimes aggression is triggered by ill-fitting shells—either too large or too small. Experiments show the aggressive tendencies of crabs as the shell fit becomes increasingly poor. (Think how aggressive we feel when our body is uncomfortable.)

Shell-fighting behavior makes sense. Hermit crabs must grow to have the advantages associated with a larger size. Growth requires larger shells. Since many populations have a limited number of shells, the only other source of a larger shell is taking one from another crab.

# Pet Hermit Crab Species

| Species/ Common Name | Habitat | Diet/ Behavior | Body Mass/ Number of Avg. Size Grapes |
|---|---|---|---|
| *Birgus latro* Coconut crab | Islands including high elevations, sand, coconut tree groves | Fruit, carrion, crustaceans, scavenges middens/ Burrows | 106 oz. (3,000 g) or 1,006 grapes |
| *Coenobita brevimanus* Indos crab | Grass, rainforests | Scavenger, omnivore/ Fills shells with fresh or brackish water | 6.5 oz. (185 g) or 65 grapes |
| *Coenobita cavipes* Concave crab | Sandy areas, lagoons | Carrion/ Prefers seawater-filled shells | 5.6 oz. (160 g) or 56 grapes |
| *Coenobita clypeatus* Caribbean/Purple pincer | Some live inland near the shore; some live in leafy dune vegetation | Omnivore; plants, carrion, feces, can be cannibalistic/ Eats plants toxic to other animals | 3.9 oz. (110 g) or 39 grapes |
| *Coenobita compressus* Pacific/ Ecuadorian crab | Inland near the shore, sand, moist and vegetated areas | Scavenger; plants, wood, fungus, carrion/ Nocturnal in arid areas; diurnal in humid areas | 1.3 oz. (38 g) or 13 grapes |
| *Coenobita perlatus* Strawberry Crab | Near the shore or dunes, tidal caves, sand, dune vegetation, humid areas | Scavenger | 2.8 oz. (80 g) or 28 grapes |
| *Coenobita rubescens* | Far inland, at high altitudes | Omnivore | 1.7 oz. (48 g) or 17 grapes |
| *Coenobita rugosis* Wrinkled crab/ ruggie/rug | Dunes, sand, dune vegetation | Algae, tortoise feces/ Hides in litter during day | 2.4 oz. (67 g) or 24 grapes |
| *Coenobita scaevola* | By the sea | Scavenger/ Burrows into litter when cold to hibernate | 2.6 oz. (74 g) or 26 grapes |
| *Coenobita spinosa* | Near the shore, dunes, and vegetation | Decaying plants and animals/ Nocturnal, burrows into litter when cold to hibernate | 1.4 oz (40 g) or 14 grapes |

*Coenobita clypeatus* uses a common form of shell fighting. The aggressor rotates and rocks the defender's shell, sometimes croaking or chirping at the same time. This combination of movement and sound sometimes convinces the defender to vacate his shell. Sometimes these fights do not result in the defender's eviction. The defender may wave his chelipeds as a threat, strike the aggressor with his chelipeds and then retreat, or remain in the shell until the aggressor leaves. These fights rarely result in physical harm to either crab.

### Noisemaking
*Coenobita clypeatus* chirps during fights with other crabs, and some defending crabs are known to make croaking and other chirping sounds. Other crabs may perceive these sounds as vibrations. Land hermit crabs are known to make these chirps on other occasions, but little study has been done on the reasons. The coconut crab also has a habit of producing clicks for reasons not clearly understood.

*Birgus latro* uses the second walking legs to make a stomping noise. Crabs also produce sounds by rubbing two body parts (e.g., legs) together. Scientists call this "stridulation." Sound produced through stridulation paired with posturing is a common method of showing aggression.

Sometimes, crabs rap their chelipeds against something resilient in the environment or against another crab's shell. For example, during courtship, the male taps his large claw on the female's shell. The meaning seems to be "come out of your shell."

### Movement and Migration
Unlike other crabs, hermit crabs typically walk in a forward motion. Many, such as *C. compressus*, move forward using a tripod gait similar to insect motion. Some Coenobitidae climb, eyes directed forward on the ascent and descent, moving upward in a spiral motion around a tree trunk. Sometimes, during descent, shelled crabs lose their grip and drop to the ground.

Land hermit crabs sometimes migrate. Females migrate seasonally to drop their ready-to-hatch eggs into the sea. *Birgus* and *Coenobita* often travel many miles (kilometers) to

## A Shell for Every Species

Experienced crab hobbyists have useful suggestions about species preference for certain types and sizes of shells. Check with one of the online groups mentioned in the Resource section to choose extra shells for your hermit species. Remember, shell preferences are usually species specific.

seawater; as a result, high numbers of otherwise seldom seen land crabs are found moving toward the ocean. Males also migrate but only for encountering females for reproduction.

One unique behavior for *C. clypeatus* on Curaçao is observed because high cliffs prevent the ready-to-hatch eggs from reaching the ocean. Scientific observers report that female crabs pull clumps of larvae with their fifth periopods, pass them to the chelipeds, and throw the larvae off the cliffs toward the ocean. Females tested in the laboratory could throw clumps a distance of up to 10 inches (25 cm).

How crabs orient toward a target is varied. Some species of crab orient toward the water, based on the slope. *C. clypeatus* can detect slopes between 0 and 2.5 degrees. Other species of hermit crab, including *C. rugosus*, use the wind, stellar navigation, and landmark recognition.

## Gathering Shells

Nearly everyone who likes the sea gathers seashells. In many areas, however, the empty shells are needed for hermit crabs and other species. Hermit crabs have evolved to be dependent on a "microhabitat" as a resource. In other words, their population is limited by the number of available shells of suitable size and condition. (Unoccupied shells in areas inhabited by hermit crabs are usually too large or too small for the local hermit crabs.)

This shortage of appropriately sized empty shells is a worldwide problem. In southwestern Madagascar, at least one species of crab—*C. rugosus*—uses fossil shells that fall from eroding coastal limestone. Crabs have also been found living in a variety of manmade objects such as plastic pill bottles and liquor mini-bottles. So, think carefully before you take shells out of the environment.

## Finding Shells

Shells protect hermit crabs from predators and dehydration. In addition, hermit crabs' eggs are protected by the shell. Larger shells do a better job of protecting their occupants. Predation rates are higher on individuals in shells smaller than the preferred size.

When a shell restricts a hermit crab's growth, the hermit crab looks for a new one. In the wild, two sources of shells are available: unoccupied shells and occupied shells. Scientists believe that although crabs will fight other hermit crabs for shells, hermit crabs do not attack the shell's original owners (snails and snail-like animals) to evict them. Of course, within our crabitats, for the health and well-being of our crabs, and to prevent aggression, we supply many times more shells for our crabs than we have crabs.

Let's look at the case of crabs choosing among empty shells, exhibiting what scientists call "fixed

# Shell Switcheroo

This hermit crab is moving into a new shell. First he moves toward the empty shell (1). Then he uses his antennae and legs to figure out if the shell is the right size, shape, weight, and has other important qualities (2). Next he backs into the shell (3). After that, the crab is sealed tightly in the shell and he can go on his way (4). Hermits switch to new shells rapidly to avoid being caught by a predator when they are vulnerable.

1

2

3

4

motor patterns." The crab examines prospective new shells with his legs in a repetitive series of movements that the crab knows from the time it hatches. This unvarying natural behavior is instinctive.

Here's the sequence of actions:

1. Chelipeds and the first pair of periopods manipulate the shell position until the opening faces the crab.
2. The crab inserts one or both chelipeds, and sometimes one or more legs, into the opening of the shell.
3. The crab examines the shell through the opening, gathering information through touch, chemical, and other sensory cues.

What kind of information is the crab gathering? One study determined that *C. rugosus* uses its chelipeds to find the internal dimensions of the shell. Another showed that for *C. scaevola*, the volume of the shell is more important than the weight. Certainly, the volume of the shell, the shape that's available to the crab for its abdomen, the room for the entire body to withdraw to escape from predators, and space left over for plenty of water is important.

After many studies, scientists have determined that a number of factors affect shell selection. *C. compressus* on the Pacific side of Costa Rica occupied 21 different types of shells. *C. scaevola* at the Red Sea occupied 12 different types of shells. The factors crabs consider include the internal volume, the weight of the shell, the size and shape of the opening, and the angle of the columnella in the shell.

## Looking at a Crab's Life

Each species of crab undergoes a somewhat different life cycle, but the general style of development is similar. Some sources state that hermit crabs can live up to ten years in captivity, while others suggest that these invertebrates can live longer than 15 years. Pet crabs are sold as adults; nevertheless, knowing about the life cycle of the crab is interesting and useful. Many hobbyists are curious about breeding their crabs. Although

### Why Are They Called Hermit Crabs?

The experts who study word origins are not in agreement with all scientists. Some scientists have said that the name comes from the use of empty shells as shelters. Another word for *shelter* is *hermitage*. The *Oxford English Dictionary* explains that the term *hermit crab* has been used by scientists since 1735 and came from the crab's habit of wandering alone, rather than in groups.

breeding crabs under excellent conditions is possible, managing the hatching and raising crab larvae is difficult. The developing crabs need an aquatic environment. In addition, successful breeders report that developing crabs must be hand-fed at each stage.

## Birth

Hermit crabs breed throughout the year. Crabs conduct a short courtship prior to mating. Females have well-developed but small legs on the left side of the abdomen, and through which eggs are laid at the base of the second pair of walking legs. The eggs are laid shortly after mating and retained until the larvae emerge. (Larvae are the free-swimming forms that will develop into crabs after several molts). Female crabs carry between 10,000 and 15,000 eggs attached to their pleopods with a "glue-like" substance. Females come partly out of their shells and fan these appendages to create water flow across the eggs to aerate them.

## Growth and Molting

The larvae hatch and molt, the mother wiping the hatchings away into the ocean using her small fourth pair of legs. These larvae grow through a series of molts lasting four or five days each to reach a stage at which they first resemble adult crabs. When the immature crab resembles the adult, he is ready to find a shell home and move onto land. The crab takes a year to reach the mature adult form. Once crabs have matured to adult form, they return to the ocean or estuary only to breed.

## Living With Hermit Crabs

The opportunity to live with a creature so unlike us is tantalizing. Part of the fun involves learning how crabs' bodies work and what makes a nurturing environment. Once you know hermit crab biology and natural history, you know how to care for your pet.

### Pet Characteristics

You may have gleaned that crabs are curious creatures who investigate their environments. Crabs do most of their feeding and moving around at night. When compared with dogs and cats, they require little care. Hermit crabs don't take well to cuddling and dressing up like a lap dog does. Crabs also don't do well outside of controlled crabitats that simulate their wild environments, and they don't adapt to rapid change.

### Space Savers

Crabs do not need more space than a dog's bed requires. However, the more crabs you have, the more space you need. One rule of thumb is at least 2 gallons (7.5 l) of tank space per crab, after an initial tank size of 10 gallons (38 l) for two crabs.

### Independent Pets

Check, feed, and water your crabs each day and do a quick pickup of uneaten food. The time of day you do your daily 10 or 15 minutes of crab chores isn't important. "Crabbers" can do a good weekly cleaning of the crabitat in about one-half hour.

Once a month, at a minimum, the crabs should be moved from the crabitat and the substrate, and everything in the environment should be washed, sanitized, rinsed, dried, and returned. How long this takes depends on the complexity of your crab environment, but plan on two hours. If cleaning takes less time, great.

Before you make a final decision about adding crabs to your life, consider carefully what the crabs need. A good way to do this is to read Chapter 2, which gives more information about the physical needs of a hermit crab.

### Handle With Care

Like most pets, crabs are individuals that vary in temperament and with their experience in being handled. Frightened crabs pinch. However, with careful handling and some feeding by hand, many crabs become interested in their keepers and react well to handling. Still, crabs remain wild creatures.

# Chapter 2

# What Hermit Crabs
# Need

Because some species of hermit crabs are inexpensive to purchase, people sometimes consider them "throwaway" pets. No animal is a "throwaway" animal. Hermit crabs are sensitive to pain, hunger, and thirst. As an exotic animal—an animal that does not normally live in an environment with people—the hermit crab has not adapted to household conditions. This means that maintaining a carefully controlled environment, one that allows the crab to feel at home, is required.

*When properly cared for, hermit crabs have life spans of 15 years or more.*

## Knowledge and Commitment

Keep in mind that crabs live for as long as 15 years. Crab care requires a few minutes each day, and more than that on a periodic basis to clean your crab's enclosure. In addition, you need equipment, such as a crabitat, lights, and proper temperature control that allows your crab to thrive. If you're unsure you have the commitment to meet hermit crabs' needs, try visiting hermit crabs or meeting hermit crab hobbyists to learn more (see Resources at the end of this book).

The decision about acquiring hermit crabs as pets is a perfect one for helping a child learn what caring for another living thing means and is a chance to learn dependability. Unfortunately, children can also learn the misconception that life is cheap. The initial cost of a hermit crab is not its value. Your investment in time and equipment to maintain an excellent home for the crab and the enjoyment and lessons learned is a better assessment of a hermit crab's value.

Land hermit crabs have specific needs that you must meet to keep your pet healthy and active. Veterinarians specializing in exotic animal care recommend that you understand how to meet the following needs for hermit crabs before selecting your crabs and the equipment you will need.

- a safe, sanitary, and uncrowded environment
- controlled temperature
- adequate substrate and plants
- water
- special needs such as for tree crabs
- air circulation
- diet

Each of these topics is considered here in detail. As you read, you can imagine the environment you could create for your crabs and further consider your feelings about a hermit crab companion.

Many hermit crab aficionados, including the Junkins family featured in Chapter 1, did not start out in this organized way. The Junkins found their first crab on the terrace of their hotel room at the beach. Many other families purchase crabs from pet stores or fairs without knowing much about them.

## A Safe, Sanitary, and Uncrowded Environment

What is safe, sanitary, and uncrowded to one creature is sandy, hot, and humid for another. Each animal needs an environment created to meet its specific needs. Hermit crabs have some unique requirements. A bit of reading and planning will ensure that your hermit crab gets the care he needs.

## Positioning Your Crabitat

Envision where in your home your crab can live safely. Your crabs should not be placed directly under or over vents and windows, which cause temperature and humidity fluctuations that can seriously harm your pets. In winter, heat

**FAMILY-FRIENDLY TIP**

### The Case Against Decorated Shells

Although they appeal to young children, painted shells are not appropriate for hermit crabs. Some crab wholesalers decorate crab shells with glow-in-the-dark flowers, cartoon characters, your favorite team's football helmets, racecars with numbers, etc. Especially for kids' rooms, painted shells seem like a good idea. In fact, painting hermit crabs' shells attracts impulse purchases.

Not only can the paint be toxic to the crab, but the paint changes the crab's ability to regulate moisture. Think how it would feel to wear a plastic suit that covered your body. You can't regulate moisture properly, and your skin wrinkles. That's what a crab experiences in a painted shell.

Finally, you don't want to see the process used to put crabs into painted shells. When it comes to decorated shells, just say no.

Hermit Crabs

not only affects the temperature but strips moisture from the air—moisture critical to your crabs' lives. In summer, air-conditioning can create drafts and cold spots, with temperatures so low that that your tank heaters will struggle. Careful crabitat placement helps avoid these problems.

You must not expose hermit crabs to activities that involve chemicals, garden supplies, or paints. For example, the garage is not a suitable place. Neither is a basement used by your model airplane–painting brother.

In choosing the right location for your crabitat, remember that hermit crabs are active at night. Light sleepers may be bothered by crabs' night activities. Also, your crabs need quiet during the day, so that they get adequate rest.

## Selecting Among Cage Types

Think through your caging decision carefully. Consider the number of crabs you wish to have and the size and shape of the space you can devote to your pets. In addition, consider who will care for your pets when you are out of town. Some crabitats can't be moved to a sitter, while others can.

To begin, consider two or three hermit crabs and a modest cage, such as a 10-gallon (38-l) aquarium. If you still love being a "crabber" after a year and want a more complex and expensive setup, you can use that first aquarium as a private molting chamber.

Keep in mind that hermit crabs need a predominantly dry environment but should have easy access to soak in the shallow water dish you supply.

If you love do-it-yourself projects, you can build a crab habitat that ranges from a basic two- or three-crab setup in an aquarium to elaborate habitats with lots of territory for roaming, natural objects for climbing, pools for bathing, and even waterfalls and misting systems. That's the beauty of being a crab hobbyist—you can use your skills and interests to benefit your crabby companions.

An ideal enclosure for a small number of hermit crabs is a terrarium with smooth sides, arranged to include an inclined gravel "beach" leading to a shallow body of water. Branches secured to prevent falling provide a place for crabs to climb. A secure lid to prevent escape is necessary.

## Vivarium

Vivariums, enclosures that provide a natural-looking setting with live plants, are popular among hobbyists who keep reptiles, amphibians, and invertebrates such as hermit crabs. Hermit crabs are well suited to a *viv*, as it is sometimes called. Land hermit crabs spend most of their time on dry land but require access to both salt and freshwater in a vivarium.

## Aquarium

Aquariums are often used as homes for hermit crabs; in fact, many hermit crab fanciers use nothing else. Specialized furnishings, such as lights and heating elements, are made for aquarium-based invertebrate care. Of course, marine hermit crabs will always live in water-filled aquariums (as fish do), but marine crabs are not a focus of this book.

## Cage Materials

Cage materials in common use are glass, acrylic, melamine, and wire.

Wire provides a cheap and flexible habitat but does not provide an effective means of moisture or temperature control. Hermit crabs should never be confined to these

### The Expert Knows

## Crabby Research

Scientists studying hermit crab behavior in the U.S. Virgin Islands learned that boat noise interferes with the crabs' response to predators. When scientists played tapes of boat motor noises, crabs were much slower to retreat into their shells when threatened by a T-shirt. (Makes you want to be a scientist, doesn't it?) We've always known that people get irritated by noisy animals. Now we know that noisy people affect animals, too.

*Hermit crabs hail from tropical climates—the one in this photo is on a beach in the Dominican Republic—and therefore need warm and humid conditions.*

and heating elements. Melamine "tanks" can be constructed to fit most any shaped space. The solid frame gives pets privacy. Most of these enclosures include a glass front.

## Size and Shape

A popular-sized aquarium is a 2- by 2- by 1.5-foot (61- by 61- by 46-cm) tank. If you have a tank that is more vertical than horizontal, then your crabs will need cage furnishings that help them use the entire cage height.

One aspect of habitat to keep in mind is the eventual adult size of your pet. According to crab expert Lindsay Renick, you need about 10 gallons (38 l) of space for every two hermit crabs in your tank.

## Cage Security

To have a secure cage, you will need to address three concerns: (1) cage stability, (2) what can get in, and (3) your crabs' escape.

As tough as their skeletons are, crabs can be badly injured by a fall or something falling on them. Place the crab cage on a strong base to ensure that the cage or tank cannot be knocked off its stand or table. Next, secure anything inside the cage, such as branches, to prevent them from toppling onto a crab.

cages except during brief periods to clean the main cage.

Glass does not scratch and holds humidity well, given a suitable lid. Acrylic is lightweight, less likely to be broken, and less expensive than glass, but it scratches.

An alternative to purchasing a vivarium is purchasing a vivarium kit to customize your own vivarium. The components usually need to be screwed together, providing a lightweight, waterproof unit made of materials such as polyethylene. Some kits include recesses for lights and heaters, allowing the unit to protect your crabs from accidental encounters of an electrical kind.

Melamine is usually a component of a larger or homemade vivarium. Melamine is easy to clean and allows holes to be drilled to incorporate light

Security means that other things cannot get into the cage. A solid-sided cage excludes mice (in search of food) as well as cats or dogs (in search of interesting, smelly things that move). Zoos often use a thin layer of petroleum jelly on the tank edges to exclude ants, lured by leftover food scraps.

Finally, ensure that your crabs cannot escape. Not only is your crab likely to be lost or stepped on, but your crab needs the special temperature and humidity of his crabitat. Because crabs are excellent climbers and are very strong, a crabitat must have a sturdy lid that has a fastener.

Eminent invertebrate culturist Dr. Frederick Frye once wrote, "Because they [hermit crabs] can leave their borrowed shells with ease, they should not be housed in bird cages... from which they can easily escape once they have shrugged out of their mobile abodes." What do you bet that Frye had this experience when he was a boy?

## Daily Cage Maintenance

Verify the proper level of temperature and humidity. Inspect your crabs to ensure that they are healthy and active. Remove uneaten food so that your crabitat stays healthy and odor-free.

### Methods for Keeping the Cage Clean

Periodically, you need to clean your entire crab habitat. To "deep" clean, remove your crabs to a safe place with adequate heat and moisture. Some crab hobbyists keep a separate tank for this purpose.

Remove everything from the tank. Wash and sanitize the bowls, climbing apparatus, and other furnishings, including the shells. Wash or replace the substrate (see "Substrates" later in this chapter) and the tank itself.

Cleaning anything an animal has contacted requires two steps: washing and sanitizing. Cleaning usually means scrubbing with soap and water until the item appears clean and all organic matter is gone. Sanitizing works only after all food and feces have been removed.

Although you can buy solutions for sanitizing, most hobbyists use

## Shells Tailor Made to Fit

How crabs select shells was a mystery until scientists investigated. One trick used by experienced "crabbers" has been to measure the largest claw. The crab should be able to retreat fully into his shell, and use the largest claw as the door.

But crabs consider other factors in shell fit. Crabs try on shells the same way you try on a new pair of jeans. They move their abdomen and tail into and out of a new shell to test it. Crabs are not opposed to used shells. In fact, sometimes crabs prefer used to new shells.

# Crabby People:
# Grant Burkhalter's Crab Castle

Not everyone wants to work as hard as Grant, but his "crab castle" shows new crabbers what's possible and may give experienced crabbers new ideas.

Grant's tank is 7 feet long by 3 feet wide by 3 feet high (213 x 91 x 91 cm). He constructed the base and frame himself. He ordered the half-inch (1.3 cm) glass from a local supplier and crafted the pond from Magic Sculpt epoxy clay.

Across the tank top, Grant installed a heating duct and an in-line fan to circulate air. A ceramic heat bulb provides heat. On the side opposite, a humidifier vents over a molting area.

Grant encourages molting crabs to dig in the special area by providing deep substrate, a privacy screen, and plant cover. A lack of climbing objects discourages other crabs from exploring there.

Crabitat substrates include coco fiber and sand. One area is all sand, another all coco fiber. The area in between provides a mix of the two. The sand next to the pond extends to a depth of 3 inches (7.6 cm). The coco fiber at the opposite end is 12 inches (30.5 cm) deep.

Color-coded dishes keep Grant from topping off with the "wrong" water. The two green dishes always contain saltwater. Tan dishes always contain freshwater.

See Grant's crabitat and crabs at www.hermitcrabcam.com, his real time "crab cam."

either vinegar or bleach. I recommend what many wildlife care centers use: bleach. Mix one part bleach to ten parts water. Wipe the bleach solution onto the tank and everything that will go back into the tank—water bowls, climbing trees, artificial plants, and so forth. Leave the solution on for at least 15 minutes. Then, rinse thoroughly with clean water. Removing all the bleach solution is important. Remember, the solution kills unwanted living things. Traces of the bleach solution are not good for your crab. When no bleach smell remains, wipe dry.

Cleaning the substrate depends on the type of substrate that you use. Sift sand to remove chunks of uneaten food. Rinse thoroughly with water and spread wet sand in a container to dry. Sand should not require replacement if you thoroughly clean it. Replace coconut bedding when rinsing no longer cleans the substrate.

### How Often Will Your Crabitat Need Cleaning?

Crabbers suggest cleaning on a regular schedule, including weekly cleanings and monthly breakdown and disinfection. If you keep more crabs in a smaller space, you need to deep clean more often.

## Temperature Control

Most hermit crabs need to be maintained between 70° and 78°F (21° and 26 °C). Maintaining the temperature requires that you (a) position your crabitat for success,

(b) monitor the temperature with thermometers, and (c) add heat, preferably using thermostatically controlled heat sources.

Cage positioning is a key strategy in maintaining crabitat temperature—not too near a window or a heating or cooling vent. Sunlight through a window can heat a small enclosure rapidly, causing your crabs severe stress or death. Think about how quickly car interiors heat up, even on relatively mild days. Now imagine packing all that heat into a space as small as your crabitat. Alternatively, if you live in a drafty apartment in Minnesota, your crab can't put on a sweater in the winter. Your tank needs to maintain a consistent temperature that mimics your crab's native habitat.

### Measuring Temperature: Thermometers

When it comes to the temperature in your crabitat, guessing is not good enough. Use at least one thermometer to measure the temperature inside. If you have a large crabitat, use two thermometers.

Thermometers come in two types, digital and analog. Digital thermometers report temperature in a digitally displayed number. Analog thermometers sometimes use a liquid that moves against a scale of numbers. When the liquid stops moving, read the temperature from the numbered scale. Either type works just fine. By the way, other analog thermometers look like dials and stick on the wall of the crabitat. Those work just fine too.

Give your crabs a naturalistic substrate that allows them to burrow, such as sand.

Install thermometers at the air and substrate levels and read them. Or use a single thermometer and take the temperature at different areas in your crabs' home.

Most pet supply stores have thermometers that adhere to the side of the habitat. You may also select a thermometer that is part of an "instrument pack" that also measures humidity.

### Thermostats as Temperature Controllers

Thermostats turn heating devices on and off to maintain a set temperature, similar to the way thermostats control your household heating system. Invest in a "central heating system" for your crabitat. Some thermostats switch heating devices on and off within a few degrees of the set temperature. Other devices work continuously, reducing the electricity supply as the temperature reaches your setting.

### Raising the Temperature

Many different devices can be used to heat your crabitat—heating pads, mats, lights, hot rocks—the variety may seem overwhelming. Although thermostatically controlled devices may be more expensive, use them to save on both electricity and stress for your crab. However, even when you use thermostatic controls, it is important to check your crabitat temperature each day. Accidents happen, and the thermostat might be turned up too high or turned down too low. It's a good idea to check before you leave for school or work and again when you return home.

## Temperature Variation Inside Your Crabitat

Another principle of captive environments is to provide a range of temperatures (within the acceptable) in the crabitat. This variety of temperatures is called a "thermal gradient." Thermal gradients allow your crabs to choose to move to warmer or cooler locations within their habitat as they feel the need.

One tip for creating this gradient is to leave a portion of the tank off the heating mat, providing a cooler end of the tank. Providing multiple locations for burrowing and climbing in the warmer and cooler tank locations allows the crab to decide what precise temperature he prefers.

## Heater Styles

Mats that look like heating pads, artificial heat rocks, infrared lamps, and lights are methods of providing heat.

### Undertank Mats

Often the best heat solution is an undertank heating pad. This works best in most situations because (1) heat rises, so undertank heat is more efficient, (2) keeping the crab away from the heat source prevents

accidental burns, and (3) using heating pads rather than lights keeps the animal from being stressed by the constant turning on and off of lights.

Undertank mats are as slim as a piece of cardboard and must be placed under your enclosure, not inside, to provide warmth in a way that will not burn your crab. Usually, these are useful only for glass-bottomed enclosures, but there are some models that work with acrylic.

### Strip Heaters and "Stickable" Mats

These types of heating elements provide "spot" heat in a container.

## Household Dangers for Crabs

Hermit crabs are more sensitive to household toxins than other pets or their human companions are. Cleaners and sprays pose hazards to your pet crabs. These include carpet and oven cleaners; furniture polish; window, bathroom, and counter cleaners; air fresheners and sanitizers; bug sprays; suntan lotions; and perfumes.

Be careful using cleaners, especially in the environment near your crabs or anywhere you allow your crabs to be. If you have questions about the substances that are toxic to your crabs, contact the ASPCA Animal Poison Control Center at www.aspca.org.

You should have several extra shells for each crab in the enclosure. It's best if the extra shells are a bit larger than your crabs' current shells.

The challenge is securing them in place. Like the larger undertank mats, always place these smaller elements on the outside of the enclosure wall.

### Infrared Lamps

Infrared lamps provide heat rather than light and do not disorient your crabs. Available in different wattages (lower wattages for smaller enclosures), you can fit them with metal reflectors to concentrate the heat in the direction of your crabitat rather than out into the room.

### Artificial Rocks

Developed for reptiles, artificial rocks with heating elements inside provide supplementary warmer locations. Separate thermostats must be used on these rocks, and they should always be placed away from the main heating source.

## Humidity Control

Crabs need high humidity that matches their natural environment. Remember, the crab's gills work only when they are moist. Hermit crabs require humidity between 50 and 60 percent actual humidity, around 70 to 80 percent relative humidity.

A properly fitting crabitat lid helps you maintain high humidity. Of course, measuring the humidity with a hygrometer instead of guessing at it is also important.

To meet your crabs' humidity needs, many methods are available to you. Dishes of water, mechanical humidifiers, special sponges, and spraying your crabs with a fine mist add humidity to your crabitat.

## Measuring Humidity

A hygrometer tells you the relative humidity of the atmosphere inside your tank. Relative humidity is the amount of moisture in the air relative to how much moisture is possible at a given temperature. Check humidity daily. Crabs' gills can't absorb oxygen without high humidity. Without humidity, crabs suffocate, even with plenty of air.

## Providing Humidity

Several methods exist for providing your hermit crab with the proper humidity. These include sponges, misting, and water reservoirs.

### Sponges

You can dampen natural sea sponges to hold water for delivering additional moisture to your crab. Despite the recommendation of pet suppliers, though, most serious crabbers believe that sponges cause more harm than good. Like the sponges in your sink, they are bacteria magnets. These bacteria can harm your crab. Many beginners use sponges to provide humidity in wire cages, inappropriate for hermit crabs under all circumstances.

If you choose to use sponges, sterilize the sponges in the microwave every day or two. Given the maintenance that sponges require, why use them?

### Misting

Misting your crab's gills (and portions of the habitat) with a fine spray of water will help keep them moist. Use a misting bottle that has only held water—if it ever held any cleaners or chemicals, the residue could harm your crabs.

### Water Reservoirs

At all times, maintain reservoirs of water, which your crab can easily crawl into and out of. One dish or pool should be saltwater. The other should be fresh. For details regarding water preparation, see Chapter 3.

## Sunlight Control

Healthy crabs require a day/night cycle. Many light systems come with timers. If yours does not, purchase a separate timer to provide a consistent 12-hour day/12-hour night cycle.

Although it does not seem to be necessary for the well-being of hermit crabs, some keepers use full-spectrum lights labeled "daylight" that mimic

# Suggested Crab Care Schedule

The family can share crab care. If kids have a calendar and sticker system for responsibilities, include crab care tasks. A chart at the tank with the chore list is another system.

Recording temperature and humidity can be fun for kids who like counting. Kids can photograph the proper food and water setup. From this, make a "flip book." Younger children can use the "flip book" to match the pictures of the food dish, the water dish, and the temperature and humidity gauges to the real objects to know whether the chores are done properly. (Are they the same, or are they different?) Older children can prepare the food, remove the uneaten food, and top off the salt and freshwater.

## Crab Care Chart

|  | Daily | Weekly | Monthly |
|---|---|---|---|
| **Food** | Replenish food | Clean food dishes | Clean and disinfect dishes |
| **Water** | Replenish water | Clean water dishes | Clean and disinfect dishes |
| **Environment** | Check substrate: should be clean, dry | Clear leftover food from substrate, wipe tank sides with moist paper towel, check substrate | Thorough cleaning: Remove everything, clean substrate, wipe down |
| **Temperature and Humidity** | Check temperature and humidity using gauges; adjust thermostats and mist as needed | Wipe gauges | Wipe and sanitize equipment; clean gauges |
| **Handling** | Handle crabs every few days to maintain tame attitudes | Consider weekly hand-feeding | Remove crabs to temporary container and secure the lid |
| **Other** | Observe each crab's general condition | Rotate shells |  |

the entire spectrum, or wavelengths, of sunlight, including the ultraviolet (UV) part that human beings can't see. If you decide to use these, mount the bulbs so that there is no glass between the bulbs and the crabs, as glass screens the UV light. However, select a light system that prevents your crabs from touching the bulbs. Putting a UV light on top of a screen cage cover usually will work fine. If you are housing your crabs with live plants, a full-spectrum light or a plant bulb will be needed to keep the plants healthy.

## Cage Furnishings

Furnishings consist of everything that goes inside the crab enclosure. The colorful "cartoonish" palm trees and beach chair furnishings that come in kits may look like fun, but those are for you to look at. Those are not the furnishings that thriving hermit crabs need. Sure, you can include a few of them for fun. What's important is what goes on the bottom of the cage, the shells your crab needs as alternative homes, and the plants you can use to decorate your crabitat.

### Substrates

The *Penguin Dictionary of Biology* defines *substrate* as "the ground or other solid object on which an animal

walks." Rocks and sand, the natural substrates found on beaches where hermit crabs live, are important components of a variable habitat for your crab. Remember that most easy-to-clean enclosures are also slippery. To make your crab comfortable, spread a substrate throughout the enclosure so that your crab can walk with ease.

Although different crab species dig to different depths, most hermit crabs have a substantial need to burrow. We'll talk more about "dig pits," so be sure to reserve a portion of your crabitat for a deep level of substrate.

Many crab care sources recommend that you create a dig pit at least twice as deep as your largest crab (and his shell) is tall. In addition, consider several substrates that mimic natural hermit crab environments: sanitized beach sand or silica-free play

*Hermit crabs climb very well and will appreciate having some branches or rocks in the enclosure on which they can climb.*

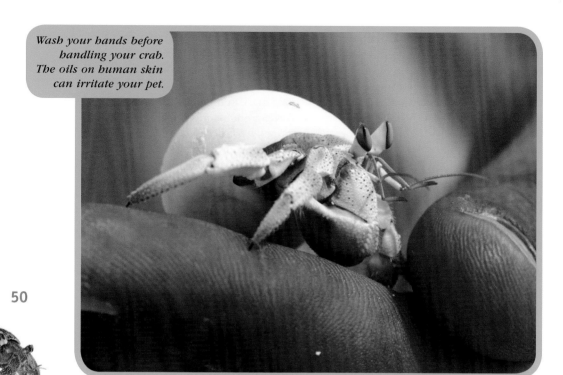

*Wash your hands before handling your crab. The oils on human skin can irritate your pet.*

sand, fine river pebbles, and crushed coral with coconut fiber that mimics the leaf litter attractive to some crabs.

## Shells

Experienced crab wranglers suggest at least three extra shells within the crabitat, available for each crab. One shell should be about the same size, and the second and third somewhat larger. Shells should not contain cracks or holes, because the water crabs gather into their shells is important to their skin health, to their respiration, and to cleansing wastes from their bodies.

Crabs use new shells because they need larger shells after molting. Some hermit crabs change shells between molts. Crabs may also switch to a larger shell before molting, owing to the soaking they do in saltwater in order to crack their cuticle in order to crawl out and burrow for the period in which they develop their new cuticle.

In summary, crabs switch shells for many reasons. Having enough shells available helps prevent shell fights, in which hermit crabs will attempt to drive less dominant crabs out of their shells in order to claim a preferred one.

## Plants

Most crabbers use artificial plants as accents for their crabitats. However, for some people, artificial doesn't seem right. Use the ASPCA website list of nontoxic plants (www.aspca.org/apcc/nontoxplants.pdf) as a guide for selecting safe crabitat decorations. Be sure that live plants have not been treated for pests with systemic poisons or fertilized with pellets that remain in the soil. These chemicals are harmful to your crabs.

## Air Circulation

Ventilation inhibits mold growth, which otherwise develops rapidly in the moist environment the crab needs. A sliding cover panel that opens to reveal screen is a good setup to circulate air in a small aquarium. Screen coverings that are completely open may not allow you to maintain proper humidity and temperature. The conditions in your home will determine whether those more open-top covers will work. If you use an open screen cover, you can place a piece of glass or plastic wrap over part of it to keep the humidity within the proper range.

## Crab Handling

Handling crabs can be fun, but you need to be gentle. You'll need to remove them for cleaning, and to be sure they are healthy. Before you pick up your crabs, let's think about the crab's body.

## How to Hold and Handle Hermits

Salt and oils on your skin can irritate or injure your crabs, so be sure to wash your hands before (as well as

## Tips from the National Zoo's Crab Keepers

Let's learn from the best— the Smithsonian's National Zoological Park's crab keepers, responsible for their *Coenobita clypeatus*. They advise keeping hermit crabs in the following conditions:

- Maintain at 75° to 80°F (23.8° to 26.6°C) and humidity above 50 percent.
- Provide freshwater in a dish large enough that crabs may soak their entire body.
- Provide climbing limbs, and sand that permits them to burrow and completely bury themselves. Add coconut litter to increase humidity and burrowing opportunities.
- Supply spare shells of different sizes.
- Feed a commercially prepared diet supplemented with bits of vegetables and fruit. Change food and water daily.
- Take care not to overcrowd your crabs. Maintain at least a 10-gallon (38-l) tank for two crabs.
- Provide a shallow bowl of saltwater for bathing and enrichment.

Thanks to Lindsay Renick for supplying this list.

What Hermit Crabs Need

# Crabby People: Robert "Glass House" Dugrenier

Glass artist Robert Dugrenier read about beachcombers collecting the empty shells hermit crabs would normally use. He wondered whether he could make hermit crab shells from glass. After 1,000 attempts, Dugrenier perfected blowing the even, thin spiral configuration of a purple land crab shell.

"Knowing how to do it doesn't make it easy," Dugrenier says. Of the 40 shells he can blow in a day, only 12 of them meet a hermit crab's exacting standards. The crabs' pickiness surprised Dugrenier. "Finding the right shell for them is like a person finding the perfect pair of jeans. You try on so many that aren't just right. But when you put the right ones on, you know it."

"The spiral structure of the shell is very strong, but a regular shell will break before glass will," he says.

Dugrenier stays close to the crab community through the Hermit Crab Association Forum (see Resources) to provide shells that meet the standards of different crab species. "Hobbyists love my shells because they can see the entire crab's body, not just the part that is usually outside the shell. See Dugrenier's shells at www. glassshell.com.

Crab in a blown-glass shell.

after) handling your crabs. Bristles, or hairs, on the crab's legs can tickle you. Be prepared for this.

Crabbers suggest handling your pets consistently, and slowly, so that your crab expects a secure environment. This reduces the likelihood of you being pinched. Keep in mind that crabs' vision is specially modified to detect movement more than focus. A slow approach works best.

In addition, the natural response to something touching the crab's claw is for the claw to pinch closed.

Always use two hands to hold your crab. Use your dominant hand (the one you write with) to support the shell at an appropriate distance above your second hand. Hold your second hand as a flat surface on which the walking legs can stand. If you allow the crab to dangle, the crab will try to steady itself with its large claw. This is a natural reaction and not an attempt to hurt the holder. In addition, although the crab has an exoskeleton, it needs to be handled firmly and never with any device that could pierce the skeleton, such as tongs.

## Dealing with an Aggressive Crab

Crabs may be aggressive toward each other or toward their human caretakers.

*Your crab must be fully supported when you handle him. If he feels unsteady, he may pinch you to keep from falling.*

Aggression has several origins. Typically, if crabs needs are met and the crab is not frightened, there is no need to be aggressive. Overcrowding, insufficient food or shells, only a single basking location that is warm enough, or fright provokes aggression.

To work with crabs that are aggressive or excessively shy with keepers, some crabbers suggest hand feeding with a special spoon or the tip of a plastic syringe. Consistent secure handling can turn an aggressive crab into a friendly one or a shy crab into one that sheds its fears.

## Dealing with a Pinching Crab

Crabs pinch when they are afraid. Crabbers suggest returning the crab to water or to a familiar substrate as a way of encouraging the crab to let go. The trick is to distract the crab with something he'd rather do.

Chapter **3**

# Feeding, Watering, and
# Bathing

Food provides the energy and raw materials for
hermit crabs to build and maintain their body
in good condition throughout their lives. Water
is also necessary for a crab's body. Crabs need
water not only for drinking but also for bathing.
Bathing keeps crabs' gills moist, which keeps
the oxygen flowing into the body and the carbon
dioxide flowing out: This is the reason bathing
and humidity are essential for crabs' health.

*Feed your hermit crab a high-quality commercial crab diet supplemented with fruits, vegetables, fish foods, and other items for variety.*

### What Crabs Eat

Wild hermit crabs travel to the shoreline daily, scavenging through dead plants and animals washed onto the beach, as well as living algae from tide pools. Like your pet crabs, wild hermit crabs are omnivores, enjoying a variety of plant- and animal-based foods. Experiments show that crabs prefer food with a different odor than that of the last meal. In addition, crabs will not eat the first thing they can scavenge unless they are very hungry. These habits and experiments suggest that pet hermit crabs prefer a variety of foods. In other words, a little of a lot of different foods rather than a lot of one or two foods.

### Commercial Hermit Crab Diets

High-quality commercial crab foods are good staple diets that contain both meat and vegetable material to feed your omnivorous crabs. In a pinch, fish food will do.

### Vegetables and Other Human Foods

In addition to a pelleted diet, provide tiny amounts of freshly prepared

## Foods Harmful to Your Crab

- alcohol or caffeine in any form
- chocolate
- cured meats
- dairy products
- sugared or salted foods

foods, such as fruits, greens, and other nonstarchy vegetables, and seafood (including those products marketed for feeding fish, such as krill and brine shrimp). Feed only small amounts to prevent overfeeding and spoilage of uneaten food.

Regardless of the food items you provide to your crabs, foods grown without pesticides are best. Of course, freshly picked food is highest in minerals and vitamins. Wild crabs may forage until they find what they need. Your crabs cannot. You must place a variety of foods within the crabitat, and from those your crabs will choose what they need.

If you provide your pets with tiny portions of table scraps, avoid foods that come from cans or boxes. Instead, provide foods that are similar to those the crab finds in nature, especially fish, leafy vegetables, and fruits. Even seaweed that you find in the grocery story (food grade) would be a good choice.

## Why Feed a Variety of Foods?

Hermit crabs stay healthy when we provide the same resources that wild crabs have available to them. Experiments show that crabs fed a varied diet grow faster and that crabs prefer to eat a variety of foods. In addition, as captive animals, one choice they have is to pick through a variety of foods presented and choose those they prefer. Selecting food is a natural behavior—and one that promotes physical and mental health for your pet.

### Activities for School-Age Kids

Parents sometimes despair at how to involve their children in the care of a pet without leaving the entire responsibility to the child. Pet care is an activity a family can share. Children can help condition water, for example, using containers the appropriate size for the child's age and dexterity. Mixing seawater involves measuring. Whether you're homeschooling your children or just reinforcing learning, let the kids create the seawater.

Another activity children can help with is selecting variety diet items. At the store, children can be sent to look for dried seaweed, ocean plankton, cuttlebone, spirulina, kelp pellets, and dried shrimp or krill. Kids can help select apples, carrots, mangoes, broccoli, bananas, chard, coconut, spinach, and grapes and share in the fun of eating these fresh foods.

Finally, older kids are great at using research skills to find answers to nutrition questions at Naturallycrabby.com and other online sources. Pets are more fun when everyone is involved.

## Feeding Made Easy

### How Often and How Much?
Provide small amounts of food daily after removing uneaten food from the previous day. This means pellets as well as fresh food, because in the moist environment, food spoils quickly.

### Crabby People: Lola Granola

Lola Granola isn't her real name, but most people in the crab world call her that. Through her websites, Hermit Crab Cuisine (www.hermitcrabcuisine.com) and Naturally Crabby (www. naturallycrabby.com), Lola collects and shares information she feels is important to the community of crabbers.

Naturally Crabby addresses the questions that vexed her when she first began crabbing (e.g., Can I keep big and little crabs together?). Hermit Crab Cuisine is all about food for crabs: What's safe and not safe?

In real life, Lola is a college professor of speech and theater and has kept (and adored) crabs for five years.

Since hermit crabs feed at night, foods left in the crabitat late in the day are apt to be fresher when your crabs dine. However, your crabs are not picky in that sense. Whether you feed at night or during the day is up to you. One advantage of hermit crabs as pets is their relative lack of dependence on your schedule. The important point is to feed them and top off their water daily.

### Use Food Bowls
Because hermit crabs are not neat eaters, the low-edged kidney-shaped feeders that allow the hermit crab to crawl into and out of the bowl help keep your crabitat cleaner. Other low-edged bowls would also be fine.

### Water: Getting it Right
Hermit crabs need access to freshwater for drinking and seawater for bathing. You need to condition your freshwater. You'll combine your freshwater and a seawater replacement mixture available from your supplier to make bathing water. More about this in a few paragraphs.

### For Bathing
In the wild, crabs bathe in freshwater and in saltwater. They bathe to keep their gills moist, to rehydrate their bodies, and to dislodge any decomposing foodstuff or feces. As odd as this seems, hermit crabs can drown if left submerged without a way to get out of their bathing chamber.

*One way to make sure your crab can get in and out of his water bowls is to put some stones that he can climb on in the bowls.*

## Water Hygiene

Keep in mind that crabs' "lack of etiquette" fouls both bathing and drinking water. Change the water frequently. Keep the bathing area remote from the food, since wet crabs moisten the substrate, which can ruin the food.

## Why Water Conditioning Is Necessary

Providing water for your crab is not a simple matter of turning on the faucet and filling the bowl. You have

Some elaborate crabitats include a "walk in, walk out" bathing facility for crabs, with a sloping substrate down to a shallow pool of saltwater. If you don't have this kind of arrangement, it's not a problem: Use a water dish or shell with sides low enough that your crab can crawl in and out. You could also use a piece of driftwood or a rock as a ladder for your crabs. Be sure to clean this regularly.

## For Drinking

Provide freshwater in containers large enough for your crabs to crawl into, yet shallow enough for them to crawl out easily. Sometimes crabs only drink the freshwater; sometimes they need a good freshwater soak.

## The Expert Knows

### Not Your Pet Crab's Diet

Some crabs that live in areas with turtles eat sea turtle eggs and turtle feces. Some crabs climb onto bushes and have been known to attack young birds. Some specialized crabs, such as the robber crab, feed on coconuts that they crack open, along with the carrion, fruits, and sago piths it prefers.

Feeding, Watering, and Bathing

## Diet Variety Suggestions

| Commercial Diet: Staple | Commercial: Other | Fruits | Vegetables |
|---|---|---|---|
| hermit crab diet | dried seaweed | mango | carrots |
| tropical fish food | ocean plankton | banana | broccoli |
| dry dog food | cuttlebone | coconut | chard |
| | spirulina | grapes | spinach |
| | kelp pellets | | |
| | dried shrimp or krill | | |

to condition your crab's water. Why? Most tap water contains chlorine or chloramines that must be neutralized before giving it to your crabs to drink or using it as the base for your seawater mixture. In addition, tap water can contain natural materials that make the water alkaline or acid. What you want is water with a neutral pH of 7.0.

### How to Condition Water
Run tap water into a clean, wide-mouthed glass or stainless steel container. Let the water remain open to air for 48 hours. This "standing time" allows the dissolved chlorine gas to escape and the water to reach room temperature.

If your water system adds chloramines to the water, you must use a chemical water conditioner to remove them. Water conditioners are available at most pet stores. Alternatively, you can purchase de-ionized or distilled water, which has no additives, such as minerals and vitamins, and which has not undergone ozone treatments.

To determine whether your water can be used after standing or whether it requires chemical conditioners, you can contact your local water utility company and ask whether chloramines are added. In addition, you can check with a good-quality local fish store. The freshwater requirements for fish are similar to the requirements for freshwater for your hermit crabs.

### How to Make Seawater
Add fresh, conditioned water to a dry seawater substitute mix. This is the same kind of salt used to make the water for saltwater fish; pet stores that sell these fish will sell the salt as well. Follow package directions as if you were preparing saltwater for fish. Store your seawater solution in a nonmetal container, as the solution

Hermit crabs need access to both fresh and saltwater at all times.

will corrode metal. Do not try to create your own ocean water using

## Why Tap Water Contains Chemicals

Many cities add chlorine or chloramines to the drinking water supply to kill bacteria, viruses, and parasites such as *E. coli* and *Giardia*. Especially after heavy rainstorms, your water district may add more chemicals to guarantee that these germs are killed. The leftover level of chemicals usually ranges from 0.5 to 2.0 parts per million, a very dilute level to you, but very harmful for your hermit crabs or fish.

table salt, because the salt in table or sea salt does not contain all the necessary elements to be an ocean water replacer.

Remember that as water evaporates from the seawater bath, the remaining mixture becomes increasingly salty. This more concentrated solution will be too strong for your crabs. If you top off your saltwater bath—instead of changing the saltwater entirely—use conditioned freshwater to keep the solution just right for your friends. Alternatively, empty the old saltwater, rinse the container, and replenish with entirely new saltwater from your prepared jug of seawater.

# Chapter 4

# Selecting Your Crab and

# Bringing Him Home

Before you commit to a crab as a pet, remember that this is not a short-lived creature. Well-cared-for crabs can live for as long as 10 or perhaps 15 years. Selecting a healthy crab starts your relationship off on the right foot. Your crab's best chance of remaining healthy is to have the crabitat established before you do your final crab selection. Conditioned water, seawater, and a supply of food make your first few days with your new pet fun rather than stressful. The more relaxed and quiet you are in your approach on those days, the better for your crab.

Select your pet from a source that maintains their crabs in proper housing and not in overcrowded conditions.

## Sources of Crabs

Hobbyists suggest selecting crabs from a pet store that also stocks items you need for your crabs' care. Knowledgeable staff, wherever you can find them, will add to your enjoyment and lower your concerns about caring for this exotic pet.

Obtain crabs from proper sources. If you're thinking of gathering your own hermit crabs, keep in mind that most hermit crabs you see on North American beaches are not the *Coenobita* species. Tide-pool-dwelling crabs require a completely different setup, usually a marine aquarium and a set of requirements so complex that zoos and aquariums

hire professional aquarists to manage the crabs' environment. If you are lucky enough to live in an area that features wild *Coenobita*, consider the value of simply observing them in their natural habitat. If you are intent on gathering local *Coenobita* as pets, check local and state regulations, which may protect the crabs from being collected or require a license before collecting them. Do your best to make sure you are collecting crabs from a healthy and stable population, not one that is declining.

The annual survey from the American Pet Products Manufacturers' Association (APPMA) reports that about one-third of hermit crabbers purchases their crabs from a neighborhood pet store; about one third purchases from fairs, carnivals, and pet superstores; and about one third purchases from other sources, including online sources.

Setting up a small terrarium—10 gallons (38-l) or so—for two crabs will be relatively inexpensive. However, more ambitious crabitats will cost more. Check with retailers and other hobbyists. Describe the setup you would like, and get their help to create a realistic budget. In addition, they can help you with ideas on what matters most when you're creating your crabitat.

I'd recommend investigating local independent pet shops first. This might be an aquarium store or simply a very good neighborhood store with a knowledgeable owner. The additional advantage is that the same source probably has excellent supplies.

One other source of hermit crabs is adopting them from someone who is discontinuing their hobby. An excellent source of this information is the Crab Street Journal Adoption Center, which offers this service as well as excellent care information, included with the other resources at the end of this book. As a new crab hobbyist, two important aspects of the source of your crab is its health and the availability of helpful information.

## How to Select Your Crab

The best way to select a healthy hermit crab begins at a reputable supplier. A fair, resort, or boardwalk kiosk is not the best place to acquire your pet. If you're adopting from a retail outlet or another crabber, the

## Setup Checklist

- Set up and position tank with secure lid.
- Condition water. Use conditioned water to create saltwater mix.
- Wash, dry, and sanitize tank.
- Wash substrate and install in tank.
- Install tank heater and set for 75°F (24°C).
- Install thermometer and hygrometer.
- Wash, dry, and sanitize water dishes.
- Wash, dry, and sanitize habitat furnishings.
- Install branches.
- Secure climbing branches so they do not fall and injure your crabs.
- Wash, dry, and sanitize additional shells.
- Purchase and store commercial diet in airtight container.
- Apply petroleum jelly around the tank top to discourage ants (optional).
- Create emergency plan, including pet sitter and veterinarian selection.
- Install sunlight bulb on timer—12 hours of light and 12 hours of darkness.
- Install humidity features, and raise humidity to 60 percent.

crab's enclosure should smell and look clean. The crabs should seem lively and should react to what is going on around them. You should see fresh and saltwater available, and what you shouldn't see are small gnats or other tiny insects around or on the crabs.

### Consider Small-Size Crabs
Crab hobbyists suggest you consider a crab size based on the tank you can provide. If you have room for a small tank, pick small crabs. Larger crabs require more space and larger essentials. In addition, large crabs are sometimes aggressive with other hermit crabs of a smaller size. Larger crabs can also pinch harder than small ones. So, if you have children, consider selecting smaller crabs that will be less apt to deliver a painful pinch.

### Consider Beginner Species
Some of the varieties of hermit crabs are more easily cared for than others are. Keeping a variety that is easy to care for is also a way of learning more about some of the varieties of arthropod that require more advanced skills to maintain. The type of crab most suitable for North American beginners is *Coenobita clypeatus* and is

most likely the one that you will find in pet stores.

### Select Lively Individuals
From the tank at your source, look for two or three of the most lively of the crabs. Conditions in stores are stressful for crabs, which are still suffering from the stress of wild capture and transport. Be sure, when possible, that your crabs have all their limbs, as already-stressed crabs have even more trouble regenerating them.

Before leaving the store, note the temperature, so that you do not shock your crabs with high heat when you return home. If the store crabitat is considerably cooler than your prepared home tank, drop your tank temperature and increase it slowly, a degree or so each hour.

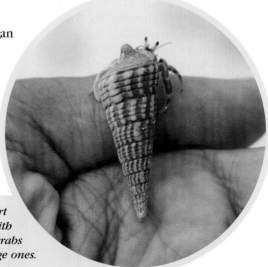

*You may want to start your crab-keeping hobby with a small hermit crab. Small crabs don't pinch as hard as large ones.*

## Prepare in Advance for Your Crabs' Arrival

It is best if you set up your crabitat well in advance of bringing your crabs home. You'll have a lot to learn, water to condition, final decisions about crabitat placement, and so forth. Making these decisions and arranging your crabs' furnishings is easier without the pressure and excitement of crabs skittering (or not skittering) around, waiting to enter their new home. In addition, setting up the temperature and humidity controls is essential.

Purchasing, installing, and learning to use your new equipment may take some time. If you have children, this is a good opportunity to explain that families shouldn't get pets on an impulse.

## Setup

Before bringing your crabs home, you should set up your crabitat, stabilize its temperature and humidity, and lay in a supply of conditioned freshwater and a jug of seawater. In addition, I suggest establishing your emergency plan.

This approach requires self-discipline, but, if they could talk, your crabs would thank you. Sorting out problems with the heater, adequate moisture, and so forth are best done before your crabs have the stress of moving from one location to another. When your checklist is complete and you have been able to maintain temperature and humidity levels for two days, you are ready to bring your pets home.

## Receiving Your New Crabs

If you are receiving your crabs by shipment, be sure to open the shipment immediately and begin caring for your crabs. Dehydration may be a problem. Take special care in handling these crabs that will have been stressed by being moved from one location to another. Remember, these crabs are also being moved from darkness into the light.

FAMILY-FRIENDLY TIP

## Planning and Shopping

Children can help create a list and gather the supplies to create your crabitat. Start with the list below and add items you need. Set your budget.

Which items do you have? Which can your kids find on Freecycle or on Craig's List? Reusing is less expensive and earth-friendly. Once you've checked off what you have and can find, then shop for the remaining items.

- Tank with secure lid
- Substrate
- Heater
- Thermometer and hygrometer
- Water dishes
- Water conditioners and saltwater mix
- Climbing branches
- Additional shells
- Petroleum jelly

Selecting Your Crab and Bringing Him Home

If you are bringing your crabs home from the pet shop, your crabs have probably already been stressed by shipment to your supplier. For this reason, many hobbyists suggest bathing your new crabs.

### Bathing Your New Crabs

Bathing crabs in freshwater when you first purchase them allows them to clean themselves and rehydrate. Provide a shallow bowl of conditioned freshwater. Caution: Do not make the bowl so deep that the crabs cannot escape. *Coenobita* can drown if forced underwater. Experienced crabbers participate in the process and use the time to check the overall condition of their crabs, including a check for mites.

## Emergency Plan

Before your crabs arrive, you want to have an emergency plan. This means selecting both a pet sitter (in case of family emergency) and a veterinarian experienced with hermit crabs.

## Veterinarians

Finding a veterinarian for your hermit crabs may not be easy. There are veterinary societies for exotic companion mammals, for fish and other marine animals, and for reptiles and amphibians. None of these exactly fits the profile of your land-based hermit crab. What to do?

Search for exotic animal veterinarians in your state or town, and begin making telephone calls.

You'll want to see a veterinarian who is knowledgeable about invertebrates.

Alternatively, contact your state veterinary schools and your state veterinary association for members who specialize in exotic animals. Try searching www.aquavetmed. info/index.cfm, checking the box for your state and the box for "Crustacean Shellfish." The contacts you make there can help you find an appropriate veterinarian.

### Pet Sitters

I recommend pet sitters who are bonded and insured and belong to a professional organization. My animals are family members and I won't leave them with nonprofessionals. The two recognized organizations are National Association for Professional Pet Sitters (www.petsitters.org) and Pet Sitters International (www.petsit.com). Each has a zip code–based sitter finder. The sitter will make a previsit and receive your detailed instructions on caring for your pets.

Another idea is to meet fellow crabbers (see Resources) with whom you can trade pet-sitting services. Keep in mind that not everyone has the same standards for pet sitting.

### Veterinary Care

Although some research has been done on veterinary care for hermit crabs, experienced crabbers know that disease often comes from inadequate care and feeding. Prevention of these few documented diseases is important, because once disease is at work, stopping the illness is often impossible.

Before introducing new crabs to your collection, isolate and health-check the new additions to prevent disease transmission. Traumatic events, such as dropping your crab or a crab fight, are inevitable; proper handling can prevent many needless events.

One important point often overlooked is crabs' vision. Hermit crabs have difficulty seeing at a downward angle. Think about how their eyes

## The Expert Knows

### Frye's Signs of Disease

- abdominal distention
- baldness (for crabs with hairy exteriors)
- impaired molting
- refusal to eat
- tiredness, inactivity, depression, lack of aggression
- unable to right himself or maintain normal body posture
- weight loss
- wounds, cuts, discoloration, or change of color

Adapted from *Captive Invertebrates: a Guide to Their Biology and Husbandry* by Frederic Frye, Krieger Publishing, 1992.

Selecting Your Crab and Bringing Him Home

*Few veterinarians are experts in crab care, but most exotic vets will see hermit crab patients.*

of the signs listed in "Frye's Signs of Disease," call your veterinarian for advice. Animals such as crabs don't usually show illness until it is advanced and the animal is very sick.

## Common Problems Requiring Veterinary Treatment

Traumatic injury suffered in falls or through accidental crushing or from fights is the most common problem seen by veterinarians. Although crabs can recover from loss of limbs, be sure you have your veterinarian look for additional injuries. For example, a hard-to-see exoskeleton injury can lead to blood loss and infections. Fatal complications arise quickly to injured crabs.

Not so hard to see is ulcerative shell disorder. Generally, this will appear as darkened areas of the shell and usually occurs after the crab has been injured in some way. The injury allows the bacteria *Beneckia chitinovora* to infiltrate the unfortunate crab. This bacteria digests the shell and is a serious illness that needs professional treatment.

Managing a molt requires recognizing the process as molting, providing adequate humidity, nutrition, burrowing space, and quiet for your crab. If your crab seems to

are arranged on the eyestalks. Crabs may not sense surface edges. Also, glass surfaces confuse crabs. (Imagine walking on a glass floor. How do you know where the edge is?)

Housing and careful nutrition are important, as is isolation from toxic chemicals. Keep in mind that as crabs roam inside or outside their crabitat, they constantly taste and smell what is in their environment with their antennae and transfer substances from their antennae and feet to their mouth.

## Signs of Illness

Daily observation of your crabs help you develop an excellent sense of what is normal for your pets. With exotic animals, the first sign something is wrong is that the animal does not act as he normally does. If you see one have trouble with his molt, this is another reason to see a veterinarian.

## The Crabby Examination
To evaluate your crab, your veterinarian will take a history of the problem, will examine your crab, and may take a culture.

### History
Describe the main problem that you noticed. When did you notice something wrong with your crab? What did you notice? Have you changed anything recently—diet, humidity, temperature? Bring a note of the current crabitat temperature and humidity. It can be helpful to bring a photo of the entire crabitat. Your veterinarian may see a husbandry issue of which you were unaware. When you make the appointment, ask if you should bring a water sample from your crab's dish or a sample of feces, and, if so, obtain instructions on how the vet prefers you store and transport these materials.

### Examination
Leave your crab in his travel container until the vet asks you to remove him. Your vet can get a sense of how your crab reacts after a period of rest.

### Cultures for Diagnosis
Your vet may take a culture to look for bacteria, fungi, or protozoa, or she may biopsy the shell or gill. She may collect blood (hemolymph) to examine it for color, clotting, and clarity. Crab blood is usually drawn

## Crabby People: You Can Become an Aquarist
If you're a fan of creatures such as hermit crabs, you might want to consider working in a related profession. That's what happened to Bruce Koike, Director of the Aquarium Science Program Oregon Coast Community College in Newport, Oregon. His passion for all things that live in or near the water led him to teach animal handling, animal health, and maintaining marine life support systems within laboratory and workplace settings. (In fact, he provided some of the information for this book.)

Because many institutions need aquatic animal husbandry workers, the Oregon Coast Community College developed the Aquarium Science Program, offering an associate's degree and certificate study programs. The first graduates, in 2005, work throughout the United States at public aquariums, fish specialty stores, research organizations, and aquaculture facilities. For more information, visit www.occc.cc.or.us/aquarium.

with a needle inserted between the two segments of the large claw.

### Diagnosis and Treatment

Your veterinarian will discuss with you possible diagnoses and treatments for your crab. These discussions may include antibiotic therapy or husbandry suggestions such as diet or assistance in relieving molting difficulties. Be sure to ask about anything you don't understand.

When treatment is prescribed, follow the directions exactly. Call to be seen again if the progress of your crab is not as your veterinarian expects.

One important question to ask is whether you need to isolate your sick crab (and for how long), or whether you will need to treat all the crabs in your crabitat. Ask whether you

need to replace your substrate and disinfect your tank.

### If You Must Give up Your Crab

Crabs live to age 10 or 15 years. Not only is releasing exotic animals into a foreign habitat cruel to the crab, who will suffer a terrible death by starvation or predation, but native wildlife can suffer. In addition, it is illegal.

The proper thing to do is to find a new home for your crab. A local teacher may be looking for classroom pets. A local nature center might be interested in displaying hermit crabs. Crab hobbyists may be interested in adopting your crab. Look for adopting parents at the Crab Street Journal Adoption Center and the Hermies Yahoo Group.

FAMILY-FRIENDLY TIP

# Teachable Moment

Purchasing a pet provides teachable moments. One moment is preparation for bringing a pet home. Encourage empathy and respect for your crabs' lives by discussing these ideas with your children as you prepare together for your new crabs:

- Hermit crabs are living things, as dogs and people are.

- Hermit crabs need their own safe places.
- Hermit crabs need food, water, and the right temperature every day.
- Who will care for the crabs each day?
- Because hermit crabs' bodies are different, we must learn special ways of handling them.

# Resources

## Natural History, Care, and Nutrition

**CoenobitaSpecies.com**
http://coenobitaspecies.com

**The Epicurean Hermit**
www.epicurean-hermit.com/

**Exotic Land Hermit Crabs**
exoticlandhermitcrabs.com

**Hermit Crab Cuisine**
hermitcrabcuisine.com/

**The Hermit Crab Patch**
www.hermitcrabpatch.com

**Wet Web Media**
www.wetwebmedia.com/index.html

## Online Hermit Crab Communities

**Hermit Crab Association (HCA)**
www.hermitcrabassociation.com

**Landhermitcrabs.com**
http://landhermitcrabs.com

## Other Hermit Crab Websites

**Hermit Crab Addiction**
www.hermitcrabaddiction.net/forum

**Hermit Crab Paradise**
www.hermitcrabparadise.com

**Hermit-Crabs.com**
hermit-crabs.com/

## Hermit Crab Blogs

**Hermit Crab Food Trials**
hermitcrabfoodtrials.blogspot.com/

**Naturally Crabby**
naturallycrabby.com/home////blog3.php

## Services

**ASPCA Poison Control Center**
www.aspca.org/pet-care/poison-control/

**Directory of Aquatic Veterinarians**
www.aquavetmed.info/index.cfm

**National Association for Professional Pet Sitters**
www.petsitters.org

**Pet Sitters International**
www.petsit.com

## Where to See Hermit Crabs

### On the Internet
**Hermit Crab Cam**
www.hermitcrabcam.com

**Monterey Bay Aquarium Hermit Crab Feeding Video**
www.montereybayaquarium.org/video/video_hermitcrab_feeding_qt.asp

### In Person
**Georgia Aquarium**
Atlanta, GA

**New Zealand Marine Studies Centre and Aquarium**
Dunedin, New Zealand

**Smithsonian National Zoological Park**
Washington, D.C.

**Monterey Bay Aquarium**
Monterey, CA

**National Aquarium**
Baltimore, MD

# References

Allen, Gerald R., and Roger C. Steene. *Tropical Marine Life*. Singapore: Periplus Editions, 1997.

Anderson, D.T., ed. *Invertebrate Zoology. 2nd ed.* Victoria: Oxford UP, 2001.

*APPA National Pet Owners Survey 2009 - 2010*. Greenwich: APPA, 2009-2010.

Aravind, Arthi. "The Care and Keeping of Your Own Dorm Pet." *The DoG Street Journal* [College of William and Mary] 14 Apr. 2010.

Barnes, David K.A. "Ancient Homes for Hard-up Hermit Crabs." *Nature* 23 Aug. 2001: 785-86. EBSCO. Web. 29 Apr. 2010.

Binns, Tristan Boyer. *Hermit Crabs*. Chicago, Ill.: Heinemann Library, 2004.

Biology. Vanessa's Land Hermit Crab Care 101. Web. 20 Apr. 2010. <http://users.tpg.com.au/users/vanessap/hermit/cs/>.

Burggren, Warren W., and Brian R. McMahon. *Biology of the Land Crabs*. Cambridge [Cambridgeshire: Cambridge UP, 1988.

Caldwell, Dave. "Is It Summer Yet? Just Ask a Hermit Crab." *The New York Times* 13 May 2007, Travel sec.

"Caring for Crabs." Caring for Crabs. *Keeping Exotic Pets*. Web. 20 Apr. 2010. <http://www.keepingexoticpets.co.uk/caring-for-crabs.html>.

Carle, Eric. *A House for Hermit Crab*. New York: Simon & Schuster for Young Readers, 1987.

"Choosing and Using Thermostats." Choosing and Using Thermostats. *Keeping Exotic Pets* (UK). Web. 20 Apr. 2010. <www.keepingexoticpets.co.uk/choosing-using-thermostats.html>.

"Decapoda (Crustacea): Anomura." *McGraw-Hill Encyclopedia of Science & Technology*. Vol. 5. New York: McGraw-Hill, 2007.

Frye, Fredric L. *Captive Invertebrates: a Guide to Their Biology and Husbandry*. Malabar, Fla.: Krieger Pub., 1992. Print.

Gender. Vanessa's Land Hermit Crab Care 101. Web. 20 Apr. 2010. <http://users.tpg.com.au/users/vanessap/hermit/cs/>.

Gherardi, Francesca, and Elena Tricarico. "Can Hermit Crabs Recognize Social Partners by Odors? And Why?" *Marine and Freshwater Behaviour and Physiology* 40.3 (2007): 201-12. EBSCO. Web. 29 Apr. 2010.

Glass Hermit Crab Shells. Taft Hill. Web. 19 Apr. 2010. <http://tafthill.com>.

Hazlett, Brian A. "Observations on the Social Behavior of the Land Hermit Crab." *Ecology* 47.2 (1966): 316-17. JSTOR. Web. 19 Apr. 2010.

"Heating Your Hermit Crab's Enclosure." Land Hermit Crab Care Guide. Vanessa's Land Hermit Crab Care 101. Web. 20 Apr. 2010. <http://users.tpg.com.au/users/vanessap/hermit/cs/>.

Hermit Crab and Whelk Animal Interview. National Aquarium in Baltimore, Aug. 2005. Web. <www.aqua.org>.

"Hermit Crab." *Columbia Electronic Encyclopedia*. 6th ed. Columbia UP, 2009. Academic Search Premier. Web. 19 Apr. 2010.

Hermit Crab Cozy. Craftster.org, 4 Sept. 2008. Web. 19 Apr. 2010. <www.craftster.org>.

HermitGuy101. "How to Make a Hermit Crab Habitat." Instructables. Web. 19 Apr. 2010. <www.instructables.com>.

HermitGuy101. "How to Make a Moss Pit for Hermit Crabs!" Instructables. Web. 19 Apr. 2010. <www.instructables.com>.

"Housing Your Hermit Crabs." Land Hermit Crab Care Guide. Vanessa's Land Hermit Crab Care 101. Web. 20 Apr. 2010. <http://users.tpg.com.au/users/vanessap/hermit/cs/>.

"The Importance of Baths." Land Hermit Crab Care Guide. Vanessa's Land Hermit Crab Care 101. Web. 20 Apr. 2010. <http://users.tpg.com.au/users/vanessap/hermit/cs/>.

Innocenti, Gianna, Allegra Bicocchi, and Marco Vannini. "The Use of Pelopods for Shell Water Circulation and Respiration by Hermit Crabs." *Marine and Freshwater Behaviour and Physiology* 37.3 (2004): 161-71. EBSCO. Web. 29 Apr. 2010.

Jensen, M. "Land Hermit Crabs Spurn Leftovers." *Science News* 153.8 (1998): 126. Academic Search Premier. Web.

"Keeping Hermit Crabs and Land Crabs." Keeping Hermit Crabs and Land Crabs. *Keeping Exotic Pets* (UK). Web. 20 Apr. 2010. <www.keepingexoticpets.co.uk/keeping-hermit-crabs-land-crabs.html>.

Kim, Mi Hyang, Sung Yun Hong, Min Ho Son, and Chang Ho Moon. "Larval Development of Diogenes Edwardsii (Decapoda, Anomura, Diogenidae) Reared in the Laboratory." *Crustaceana* 80.9 (2007): 1071-086. EBSCO. Web. 29 Apr. 2010.

Kurta, Allen. "Social Facilitation on Foraging Behavior by the Hermit Crab." *Biotropica* 14.2 (1982): 132-36. JSTOR. Web. 19 Apr. 2010.

Land Hermit Crab Care Guide. Vanessa's Land Hermit Crab Care 101. Web. 20 Apr. 2010. <http://users.tpg.com.au/users/vanessap/hermit/cs/>.

"Land Hermit Crab." Think Tank. Smithsonian National Zoological Park. Web. 20 Apr. 2010.

"Land Hermit Crabs from around the World." *The Crab Street Journal.* Web. 20 Apr. 2010. <http://users.tpg.com.au/users/vanessap/hermit/cs/>.

Lerner, K. Lee., and Brenda Wilmoth. Lerner, eds. "Crabs." *The Gale Encyclopedia of Science*. 3rd ed. Vol. 2. Detroit: Gale, 2004. 1091-092.

Lewbart, Gregory A. *Invertebrate Medicine*. Ames, Iowa: Blackwell, 2006.

""Live" Vivarium/Terrarium-with Photos- How I Did It." Hermies: Land Hermit Crab Owner's Society. Yahoo Groups, 29 Nov. 2004. Web. 19 Apr. 2010. <http://pets.groups.yahoo.com>.

Mann, Adam. "'Cryptic Species' Offer Scientists a Window into Evolution." *The Mercury News.* 9 May 2010. Web. 11 May 2010. <www.mercurynews.com>.

Millius, Susan. "Human Noise May Distract Animals." *Science News* 177.6 (2010). Academic Search Premier. Web. 15 Apr. 2010.

Mitchell, K. A. "Competitive Fighting for Shells in the Hermit Crab, Clibanarius Vittatus." Aggressive Behavior 2 (1976): 31-37. EBSCO. Web. 29 Apr. 2010.

Reed, Rachel, and Erin Baxter. Invertebrate Husbandry and Nutrition. Resources for Zoological Medicine Foundations Course. North Carolina State University Libraries, 19 June 2010. Web. 30 Apr. 2010. <http://www.lib.ncsu.edu/vetmed/research/zoohusbandry.html>.

Rough, Bonnie J. "Notes on the Space We Take." *The Best American Science and Nature Writing 2007*. Boston: Houghton Mifflin, 2007. 178-85. Print.

Safe Handling. The Hermit Crab Patch. Web. 4 May 2010. <www.hermitcrabpatch.com>.

Seashell Selections. Vanessa's Land Hermit Crab Care 101. Web. 20 Apr. 2010. <http://users.tpg.com.au/users/vanessap/hermit/cs/>.

Strauss, Robert. "Own a Hermit Crab? It Probably Came from Here." *The New York Times* 13 Aug. 2000, New Jersey and Company sec. Print.

"Using Heaters and Thermometers." Using Heaters and Thermometers. *Keeping Exotic Pets* (UK). Web. 20 Apr. 2010. <www.keepingexoticpets.co.uk/using-heatersthermometers.html>.

"Vivarium, Terrarium or Aquarium; What's the Difference?" *Keeping Exotic Pets* (UK). Web. 20 Apr. 2010. <www.keepingexoticpets.co.uk/vivarium-terrarium-aquarium-whats-difference.html>.

Weis, Judith S. "Studies on Limb Regeneration in the Anomurans Pagurus Longicrapus and Emerita Talpoida." *Journal of Crustacean Biology* 2.2 (1982): 227-31. JSTOR. Web. 29 Apr. 2010.

"What Do Hermit Crabs Eat?" Land Hermit Crab Care Guide. Vanessa's Land Hermit Crab Care 101. Web. 20 Apr. 2010. <http://users.tpg.com.au/users/vanessap/hermit/cs/>.

"What Is Humidity?" Land Hermit Crab Care Guide. Vanessa's Land Hermit Crab Care 101. Web. 20 Apr. 2010. <http://users.tpg.com.au/users/vanessap/hermit/cs/>.

# Index

Boldfaced numbers indicate illustrations.

Index

## Acknowledgements

Thank you to TFH Publications, particularly Tom Mazorlig, and to Kate Epstein, Epstein Literary Agency. Thanks also to those who assisted with research and answered my many questions including: Grant Burkhalter, Dr. Elizabeth Demaray, "Lola Granola", Laurie Junkins, Elizabeth Massa-MacLeod , Multnomah County Library's extraordinary librarians, Robert DuGrenier Associates Inc. (Robert DuGrenier), the Oregon Coast Community College (Bruce Koike, Director, Aquarium Science Program), the Smithsonian National Zoological Park (Lindsay Renick Mayer, Office of Public Affairs), Carl Wilson

## About the Author

Carol Frischmann holds a B.S. in Science Education from Duke University and has written four books on animals and ecology. A member of the National Science Writers Association, she has worked in wildlife rehabilitation facilities for many years. A cranky parrot and a hyperactive Doberman Pinscher closely supervise Carol's work in her Portland, Oregon office.

## Photo Credits

Absolute Images Fine Photography: 80
Annetje (from Shutterstock): 16
Mari Anuhea (from Shutterstock): 72
Joan Balzarini: 46, 53, 59 (top)
Joel Blit (from Shutterstock): 14
Grant Burkhalter: 42
Chris Burt (from Shutterstock): 22
Castro Luis (from Shutterstock): 68
Colette3 (from Shutterstock): 12
Michiel de Wit (from Shutterstock): 47
Kushch Dmitry (from Shutterstock): 15
Robert Dugrenier: 52
Euro Color Creative (from Shutterstock): 36
Jose Gil (from Shutterstock): back cover (bottom)
Haveseen (from Shutterstock): 19, 40, 54
IrinaK (from Shutterstock): 32
Eric Isselee (from Shutterstock): 24, 60
Nancy Kennedy (from Shutterstock): 62
Sergey Khachatryan (from Shutterstock): 6, back cover (top)
David W. Leindecker (from Shutterstock): 70
Daleen Loest (from Shutterstock): 4
Loskutnikov (from Shutterstock): 50
Myroslav Orshak (from Shutterstock): 8, back cover (top center)
Photogerson (from Shutterstock): 66
Qingqing (from Shutterstock): 3, 9
RCPhoto (from Shutterstock): 20
Jason Patrick Ross (from Shutterstock): 73
Elzbieta Sekowska (from Shutterstock): 7
Supachart (from Shutterstock): 34
Aleksandar Todorovic (from Shutterstock): 44
Maleta M. Walls: 26, 30 (all)
Shi Yali (from Shutterstock): 25